PENNIES AND POSSIBILITIES

On Air Book 4: A Small Town, Second Chance, Sweet, Office Romance

Kel Summers

Copyright © 2024 Kel summers

All rights reserved

The characters and events portrayed in this book are fictitious. Any similarity to real persons, living or dead, is coincidental and not intended by the author.

No part of this book may be reproduced, or stored in a retrieval system, or transmitted in any form or by any means, electronic, mechanical, photocopying, recording, or otherwise, without express written permission of the publisher.

For permission requests, contact Kel Summers at hello@KelSummers.com.

Cover design by Kel Summers using resources from Canva Pro and/or Microsoft Design Image Creator and/or DALL-E.

Contents

Title Page
Copyright
Free Gift
Special Invitation
Introduction — 1
Chapter One — 3
Chapter Two — 9
Chapter Three — 15
Chapter Four — 21
Chapter Five — 27
Chapter Six — 37
Chapter Seven — 47
Chapter Eight — 53
Chapter Nine — 57
Chapter Ten — 65
Chapter Eleven — 71
Chapter Twelve — 75
Chapter Thirteen — 81
Chapter Fourteen — 93
Chapter Fifteen — 103
Chapter Sixteen — 113
Chapter Seventeen — 119
Chapter Eighteen — 125

Epilogue	131
Dear Reader	139
About Kel Summers	141
Books by Kel Summers	143

Free Gift

For updates, sneak peeks, release dates, news, and more, sign up to receive Kel Summers' newsletter and receive your FREE copy of Silent Sunsets.

Or sign up at https://bookhip.com/CLSQHDV

Special Invitation

Join Kel Summers VIP Beach Retreat Romance Book Club and be the first to know about new releases, updates, and secret giveaways.

https://www.facebook.com/groups/1294702547799834

***

Follow Kel Summers on Facebook.

https://www.facebook.com/KelSummersRomanceAuthor/

***

Follow Kel Summers on Amazon and get notified of upcoming new releases.

https://www.amazon.com/stores/Kel-Summers/author/B0C74QG5L7

***

Follow Kel Summers on BookBub

https://www.bookbub.com/authors/kel-summers

***

Follow Kel Summers on GoodReads.

https://www.goodreads.com/author/show/39592277.Kel_Summers

INTRODUCTION

When the past demands to be erased, can Penny find the courage to rewrite her future?

Everything Penny thinks she knows about love, career, and herself is about to be tested. After a painful breakup with Nathan, the man who walked out of her life without a backward glance, Penny is left not just with a shattered heart but also a life in pieces. As she grapples with the fallout of Nathan's departure and his shocking legal demands to erase all traces of their time together, Penny finds herself at a crossroads.

With her radio show thriving on sarcasm and self-deprecating humor, she begins to wonder if it's time for a change. Can she break free from the cycle of negativity that has defined her career, or will her audience resist the shift toward something more empowering? With the support of her friends, Penny is determined to reclaim her life, but the path forward is far from easy.

As Penny faces the challenge of reinventing her show and herself, she's forced to confront a brutal truth and ask herself some tough questions.

Can Penny truly move on from Nathan and the past that

haunts her? And more importantly, can she find the strength to rewrite her story, even if it means losing everything she thought she wanted?

Will Penny finally take control of her future, or will her past hold her back, casting a shadow over the happiness she deserves?

CHAPTER ONE

The night felt colder than usual as Penny sat alone on her couch, cradling a steaming cup of tea in her hands. The silence of her living room was deafening, broken only by the faint hum of the refrigerator and the occasional car passing outside her window. The twinkling lights of the distant skyline across the bay seemed to mock her, each one a tiny reminder of the hope she was struggling to hold onto.

Most days, Penny managed to keep her spirits up, finding moments of joy and feeling like she was on the right path. But then there were the days when the weight of it all would catch up to her, and she found herself grappling with the same unanswered questions that had haunted her since Nathan left. Weeks had passed since he walked out of her life, yet the memories still played on a loop in her mind, each one a reminder of the closure she never got. The happiness she'd felt after that cathartic night of karaoke with Mark and Stacie had been fleeting, a brief reprieve before the reality of her situation settled back in. Now, each day felt like a balancing act, where even the slightest misstep could send her tumbling back into the abyss that she was trying so hard to crawl out of.

Slowly, but surely, the team was turning things around on the radio show. But it was apparent to everyone that the show didn't have the same appeal as it once did. Penny could see it in the way Jake hesitated before pitching new ideas, the way Chloe's cheerful demeanor had started to wane, and the way Walter's encouraging words felt more like a plea for something to change. They were all walking on eggshells, and Penny couldn't help but wonder how much longer Ted or even Ruth would let them continue like this before the inevitable ultimatum came.

Ruth had been conspicuously absent since Nathan's sudden departure. Penny had half-expected a call or an email, some acknowledgment of the situation, but instead, there had been silence. She'd heard whispers that Ruth's husband, William, was in poor health, and a part of Penny wondered if that was why Nathan had been allowed to slip away so easily, and without any consequences. She'd never worked with family, and she could only imagine the tension of balancing personal and professional responsibilities and the drama that unfolded behind the scenes.

Penny's thoughts were interrupted by the sudden buzz of her phone on the coffee table. She reached for it with a sigh, ready to swipe away another generic notification. But it wasn't a promo or a reminder. It was a text from Daphne. She hadn't talked to Daphne since the day she'd shown up on Penny's doorstep with a box of her things that Penny had left at Nathan's apartment. Penny's heart skipped a beat, and her breath caught in her throat as she read the message:

> **Daphne:** *I debated whether I should tell you or not, but if it were me, I'd want to know. Nathan will be back in*

town tomorrow, at least for the day.

Penny stared at the screen, her fingers hovering over the keyboard as if typing a response might pull her back into the tangled web Nathan had left her in. The words seemed to pulse with an intensity that filled the room, drowning out everything else.

Nathan was back in town. The thought sent a jolt of something electric through her—a mixture of hope, fear, and something else she couldn't quite name. She typed a quick *thank you* and then fought the urge to fling her phone across the room, settling instead for dropping it back on the table as if she were playing a game of Hot Potato.

Now, sitting in the quiet of her living room, she didn't know what to do with the information. If Nathan wanted to see her, he would have told her himself. But he didn't. And his silence continued to speak volumes.

The silence pressed in around her as her mind raced with questions, each one leaving her more confused than the last. *What was he doing back in town? Was it for business, for pleasure, or something else entirely? Would he reach out to her? And most importantly, if he did reach out, did she even want to see him again?*

The truth was, she wasn't sure she could handle it. Penny knew she had to protect herself. She couldn't keep hoping for a reconciliation that might never come. But the pull to see him, to understand and get some closure, was strong. Stronger than she wanted to admit.

❖ ❖ ❖

Penny's thoughts were still jumbled when she pulled up to the radio station the following morning. And despite the station's bright lights and familiar hum when she walked in, the studio felt emptier than usual, as if the energy had been drained from the room. She moved through the motions of the show, her face set in a practiced smile as if she were on autopilot. Her jokes landed, and her timing was perfect, but she knew she was phoning it in.

Chloe glanced over at Penny, a crease of concern forming between her brows. As the show continued, it was as if Chloe was holding her breath, waiting for something that never came. Penny tried to ignore it, but the weight of her thoughts made it impossible to shake off. Finally, as Jake flipped the switch to end the broadcast, he turned to her, folding his arms across his chest.

"Hey, you okay?" he asked, searching her face. "You've been pretty quiet this morning."

Penny managed a weak smile. "Yeah. I've just got a lot on my mind."

Jake held her gaze for a moment longer, then nodded. "Well, if you need anything, you know we're here."

Jake didn't press further, but she could tell he was worried. And she couldn't blame him. She'd been a shadow of herself these past few weeks as she struggled to regain her footing in a world that seemed to have shifted beneath her.

Penny gathered her things, stuffing papers and notes into her bag with a sigh, when Chloe sidled up next to her, nudging her lightly with an elbow. "Alright, spill it. You've been acting like you're a million miles away."

Penny hesitated, chewing on her lip as she thought about how much to share. She'd been leaning on Chloe and the rest of the team for weeks, and a part of her feared they were getting tired of hearing about Nathan. Then again, she could always count on Chloe for a healthy dose of honesty.

She sighed, "I found out last night that Nathan's in town. I've been debating whether I should try to see him. I mean, I know I should probably just get over it. Right? I mean, it's dumb to keep hoping for something that isn't there."

Chloe's expression softened as she reached over and squeezed Penny's hand. "You'll get over it when your heart is ready. If you feel that you need to see him, then maybe that's what you need to do. But…" She tilted her head and gave Penny a thoughtful look. "maybe consider what happens when you are face-to-face. And ask yourself what you're hoping for. What's the outcome you're looking for here?"

Penny looked away, swallowing the lump in her throat. What did she hope for? The truth was painfully simple. She wanted Nathan to see her, to realize that leaving had been a mistake, to come back and promise never to walk away again. But she couldn't bring herself to say that out loud, not even to Chloe.

Instead, she shrugged, her gaze fixed on the floor. "I don't know. Part of me wants to see him, but… what's the point? He's in town, and he hasn't said a word. If he wanted to see me, he would have reached out by now."

"Maybe he's waiting for you to make the first move," Chloe suggested, though there was doubt in her voice.

Penny let out a bitter laugh, shaking her head. "Or maybe he's just done," she replied, her tone sharper than she intended. "And maybe I should be, too." She took a deep breath, trying to calm the sudden surge of bitterness that caught even her by surprise.

Chloe studied her for a moment before speaking again, her tone gentle but firm. "Look, seeing him might be the closure you need. Sometimes, holding onto someone is more about protecting yourself from grieving. You might see him and realize he's not as important to you as he once was."

Penny snorted, though a genuine smile tugged at the corner of her lips. "When did you get so wise? And why aren't you offering relationship therapy somewhere?"

Chloe hopped up from where she was perched on the corner of Penny's desk. "You're right. I should start charging for my little gems of wisdom."

Penny rolled her eyes, and the tension in her shoulders eased up just a bit. "Come on, let's get out of here," Penny said, standing up. "I'll buy you lunch if you promise not to start charging me an hourly rate."

As they walked toward the corner deli, Penny felt a slight lift in her spirits. The fresh air and sunshine definitely did more for her than the stifling walls of the studio ever could.

CHAPTER TWO

The two women settled at their usual table on the deli's patio. As they waited for their orders to arrive, Penny sat quietly, lost in thought, her gaze fixed on the steady stream of people passing by their table. When their server arrived and placed their salads in front of them, Chloe broke the comfortable silence that had settled between them.

"I could always go with you to see him. We could make it a proper stake-out. You know, very stealth and very dramatic. Plus, I'd be there to stop you from running him over with your car."

Penny snorted, nearly choking on her water. "You know, it's scary how you can read my mind like that," she said as she wiped her mouth, laughing at the sheer absurdity of Chloe's suggestion. They often joked about watching too much *Snapped* and *CSI*, claiming they could have a brilliant career in criminal activity if they ever decided to cross that line.

"But serious, would you really come with me?" Penny's voice was a mix of hope and uncertainty. "I realize this might be a whole new level of crazy, so having someone there with me while I basically stalk him actually makes me feel a little bit better about it."

"Why not?" Chloe shrugged, unfazed. "Besides, it's not every night that I get to drive around crazy town with you. And if a stake-out is what it takes to help you figure out things on your end, then count me in."

Penny felt a warmth spread through her chest, a hint of relief loosening the knot that had been sitting there since she received the news that Nathan was back in town. She looked down, trying to hide the emotions that were threatening to spill over. "Thanks, Chloe. I don't know what I'd do without you. Really."

"Probably run Nathan over with your car," Chloe replied dryly, sending them both into another fit of laughter.

When they finally composed themselves, Penny pushed her empty plate aside, settling back in her chair with a long exhale. She looked at Chloe, who was studying her with a raised eyebrow.

"What's up? Chloe asked. "You look like you just let go of something heavy. Are you feeling better?"

"Honestly?" Penny said, running a hand through her hair. "I think I did. I've been stuck in my own head, overthinking everything. Just talking it out with you, making these ridiculous plans—it's like I can finally breathe again."

"That's what friends are for," Chloe replied with a smile. "So, what's next?"

Penny reached for her phone, her fingers hovering over the screen before typing a quick message. "I'm texting Daphne to see what Nathan's schedule looks like today. If he's got a gap, I'm going to try to catch him."

Chloe's face softened, a mixture of concern and curiosity in her eyes. "Whatever you decide to do, I'm all in with you, But..." she paused. "Are you sure about this? What if he's not ready to talk? What if... what if he doesn't want to see you?"

"I'm not sure about anything," Penny admitted, hitting send and setting the phone back on the table. "But I need to know that I tried. Whether it's for closure or something else. Whatever it is, I can't keep wondering."

They sat in silence as the minutes ticked by, each one stretching longer than the last. Penny kept glancing at her phone, the anticipation building with each passing second. Finally, her phone buzzed, and her heart did a little flip as she picked it up to read Daphne's reply.

"His last meeting should be over by 3. They're running pretty close to schedule," she read aloud.

Chloe leaned in, her eyes searching Penny's face. "So, you're really going to do this?"

Penny couldn't help the small smile that tugged at her lips, though she quickly tried to temper her excitement. "Yeah. I think I am. I just need to go into this with an open mind. It's not like I'm expecting anything to change. However, it would be nice if I saw him and felt... nothing. Maybe just a little annoyed that I wasted so much time on him and that he wasn't worth all those sleepless nights."

"That sounds like a win to me," Chloe said, matching her

smile. "So, what's the plan?"

"We'll head out after work," Penny decided, her voice firming up with resolve. "That should give us plenty of time. I want to be calm and clear-headed when I see him. No distractions."

Chloe gave her a nod. "That sounds like a solid plan. Just remember, no expectations. Whether it's closure or... something more, you've got to be ready for whatever happens."

"You're right. No expectations, just... closure." Penny nodded in agreement as she checked her watch. It was a little past noon. She had a couple of hours to plan her next move, to decide exactly what she would say to Nathan when she saw him.

Back at her desk, Penny stared blankly at her computer screen, her fingers hovering over the keyboard. To anyone walking by, she might have looked deeply engrossed in a news article, when in reality, her mind was miles away, running through scenarios, plotting the best place to intercept Nathan.

The most likely spot, she figured, would be the private airstrip where his family's jet waited. She knew access to that side of the airport would be nearly impossible without a pass. So, if she were serious about confronting him, she'd need to catch him as he left the newspaper's office. But... what if she could get her hands on an airfield pass? The thought of it sent a spark of anticipation racing through her.

She glanced toward Ted's office, which was empty. She

remembered him mentioning something about a lunch meeting with a potential advertiser, and she knew that he and Jake wouldn't be back for a couple of hours.

Penny's gaze lingered on the open door, a half-baked plan beginning to form. She knew exactly where Ted kept the passes. She had seen him pull them out of his top drawer when she'd gone with Chloe to pick someone up from the private airstrip once before. The thought of taking one of the passes without permission sent a shiver of apprehension down her spine. But the urge to see Nathan and finally get the answers she craved was too strong to resist. And this might be her only chance.

The temptation was overwhelming, a siren call she couldn't ignore. She rationalized it as harmless She would just take a quick look to… make sure the passes were still there… just in case she needed to borrow one. Besides, she'd been through so much already. Didn't she deserve some answers? Penny took a deep breath, pushing back her hesitation.

With her pulse quickening, Penny quietly stood up from her desk and walked into Ted's office, slipping inside as quietly as she could.

Except for the low hum of the air conditioning, the room was eerily silent. She could almost hear the blood rushing in her ears as she approached his desk. The drawer slid open smoothly, and her trembling fingers fumbled through the contents, rifling through papers and office supplies until her eyes landed on the familiar airport logo. There they were.

Penny froze, her hand hovering over the passes. She glanced

back at the doorway, her stomach tightening, half-expecting to see someone standing there, catching her in the act. But the hallway and the station beyond remained quiet. It was now or never.

Steeling herself, she snatched up a pass and slipped it into her pocket, feeling a surge of adrenaline as she did. Quickly, she closed the drawer, straightened, and took one last look around before retreating to her desk, her heart pounding. She could almost hear her gran's voice reminding her about karma, but she brushed it aside. She'd deal with the consequences later. Right now, she had a plan.

CHAPTER THREE

Two hours later, Penny and Chloe sat in Penny's Jeep, parked across from the newspaper office. Penny had discreetly backed into a parking spot that gave them a clear view of the entrance to the building. Penny's heart drummed a steady rhythm of anticipation as they waited.

"Are you sure about this?" Chloe asked again, her voice gentle and laced with concern.

Penny kept her eyes on the building's entrance, fingers tapping anxiously on the steering wheel. "I'm not sure of anything right now," she admitted, her voice betraying the tension she tried to mask. "But I have to see him, Chloe. I need to hear him say that this is really the end."

Chloe nodded, understanding etched in her face. "I get it. Just… remember why you're here. This is for you… not him."

A faint smile tugged at Penny's lips. "Thanks, Chloe. Really. For everything." She felt the gratitude swell in her chest, appreciating Chloe's support more than she could express.

They fell into a comfortable silence. Both women were lost in their thoughts as they watched the entrance, waiting for

Nathan to emerge. Penny's grip tightened on the steering wheel, and her eyes flickered between the double doors of the building and the clock on the dashboard, counting down the minutes with each anxious glance. She imagined all the different ways this could go, her mind spinning with possibilities, none of them reassuring.

As the minutes dragged on, Penny's anticipation gnawed at her resolve, and she started to question whether this was the right move. The digital display on the dashboard finally flipped to 3:00, and both women straightened in their seats, their eyes locked on the door.

"There! Is that—?" Penny's breath caught as a group of employees exited the building, chatting casually as they strolled past.

She slumped back in her seat, letting out a frustrated sigh. "False alarm."

Chloe reached over and gave her arm a reassuring squeeze. "Don't worry. He'll be out soon."

They waited, the silence in the Jeep thickening as the minutes ticked by. Finally, at nearly a quarter past, the door swung open again. Penny sat up, hand hovering over the door handle, ready to jump out. But again, it wasn't him. She let out another sigh, glancing at Chloe with a wry smile.

"Of course, his last meeting would run late," she muttered, trying to keep her tone light, though the frustration was evident.

"Maybe text Daphne, just to be sure we didn't miss him?"

Chloe suggested. "It's unlikely that we did. But I'd rather be safe than sorry."

Penny's hands shook as she typed out the message. She knew they hadn't missed him, but she needed confirmation. She stared at the screen, watching the three little dots that indicated Daphne was typing a response. Penny's heart pounded in her ears as she waited.

Daphne's reply came through, and Penny's stomach dropped as she read it.

> **Daphne:** *His last meeting was moved to the print shop. They said he left about ten minutes ago. He's heading to the airport now.*

Penny groaned, thrusting the phone toward Chloe. "He's already on his way to the airport."

Chloe scanned the message and then handed the phone back. "Okay, well, we know where the airport is," she said. "So, let's go!"

"Chloe, wait. There's something you should know. Nathan flies on the family jet from a private airstrip. We won't be able to get close without using this…" Penny hesitated, pulling the press pass from her pocket and showing it to Chloe.

Chloe's eyes widened. "Is that one of the press passes from the station?"

"Yeah," Penny nodded, a guilty look flickering across her face. "I, uh… may have borrowed it from Ted's desk. I didn't tell you about it because I don't know if it'll get us in trouble, and I don't want you dragged into this."

Chloe shrugged, offering a reassuring grin. "Too late for that now. And who knows? We don't even know if we'll have to use it. The pass might be expired, or maybe Daphne's timing is off, and he's already on the plane. But we won't know until we get there."

Penny nodded, feeling a mixture of dread and determination swirling in her chest. Chloe was right—maybe they wouldn't have to use the pass. She checked both ways before pulling onto the main road, her foot pressing a bit harder on the gas than usual.

The drive to the airport felt tense and surreal, and every passing second felt like a race against time. Chloe tried to fill the silence with light conversation, but Penny could only manage brief responses, her mind too preoccupied with what she might say when she finally saw Nathan. Her heart pounded in her chest, each beat echoing the growing uncertainty this confrontation might bring.

When they reached the entrance to the private airstrip, Penny glanced at Chloe, who gave her a supportive nod. Penny held up the pass to the guard, her hand trembling slightly. The scanner beeped, and a moment later, the gates swung open, granting them access.

"We're in," Chloe whispered, a mixture of excitement and apprehension in her voice.

Penny gripped the steering wheel so tightly her knuckles turned white, the tension in the car thick enough to cut with a knife. "Now all we have to do is find him," she muttered, more to herself than to Chloe, who was scanning the buildings with equal intensity.

They circled the first two buildings, the silence between them broken only by the occasional crunch of gravel under the tires. The empty hangars loomed like silent sentinels, offering no clue where Nathan might be. But as they approached the third building, Chloe suddenly leaned forward, her eyes widening.

"There! Is that him?" Chloe's voice was hushed, but the urgency in her tone was unmistakable. She pointed to a figure standing by a sleek black car, watching the man beside him pull a bag from the trunk.

Penny's heart jumped into her throat as she followed Chloe's gaze. It was Nathan, unmistakably him. The sight of him after all these weeks sent a jolt of emotions through her. Without thinking, she parked and climbed out of the Jeep. Chloe followed close behind her.

Nathan turned. His expression was unreadable as he caught sight of them. He shielded his eyes from the setting sun, and Penny felt a surge of something—anger, longing, and something she couldn't quite name—as she faced him. Chloe stayed by her side, silent support radiating from her presence.

Nathan's eyes narrowed, his posture stiffening as he watched Penny approach. The driver handed him the last of his bags, but Nathan barely noticed, focusing entirely on the two women standing before him.

KEL SUMMERS

CHAPTER FOUR

"Penny. What are you doing here?" Nathan's voice was sharp, each word cutting through the air with an edge that caused Penny to flinch. "Are you following me?"

Penny felt the sting of his tone like a slap, causing her words to catch in her throat. She had pictured this moment so many times, but none of her imagined scenarios had prepared her for the icy wall he was putting up now. She took a shaky breath, struggling to keep her voice steady, but it faltered under the intensity of his gaze.

"Nathan, I just…" she began, her words fumbling as she searched for the right thing to say that would break through his defenses.

"No," he interrupted, his voice harsh and unrelenting. "You need to answer me. Right now. How did you even get in here? This is a private airstrip."

It was as if the ground beneath her had shifted, leaving her off balance. The sharpness of his words—the sheer force behind them, left her reeling. No one had ever spoken to her like that, and she fought the urge to snap back, to knock him down a few pegs.

Instead, she exhaled slowly, trying to regain her footing, choosing her words carefully.

"The station has a pass," Penny explained, her voice trembling. "I tried to see you at the newspaper office. I just wanted to give us one last chance or at least say a proper goodbye. I know you were scared by how close we were getting. I just... Nathan, we can take this one step at a time. I needed you to know that. I can wait until you're ready."

Nathan's expression hardened, his eyes narrowing to slits, ignoring her plea. "So, you used the station's pass to ambush me? That's a violation of the agreement my attorney sent over," he snapped, his voice cold. "I don't understand why you just can't accept that we're over. It doesn't matter how I felt or still feel. I'm in Seattle now. I've moved on."

His words hit her like a punch to the gut. "Wait... still feel?" she repeated, grasping onto the slip like a lifeline. "If you still feel something, why are you doing this?" Her voice cracked, desperation leaking through her defenses. She searched his face for any sign of the man she'd known, but he looked at her with eyes as cold as steel.

Nathan shook his head, a slow, deliberate motion that felt final. Without another word, he turned on his heel and walked away, the distance between them growing with each step. Penny stood frozen, watching as he boarded the plane without a backward glance, the door closing behind him with a finality that left her breathless.

Chloe was suddenly at her side, an arm wrapped around

her shoulders, pulling her into a warm embrace. "I'm sorry, sweetheart," she murmured, her tone soft and filled with concern.

Penny's gaze stayed fixed on the plane. Her heart felt like it had been shredded into a million pieces, each fragment cutting deeper than the last. "I just don't get it," she whispered, her voice breaking as tears filled her eyes. "I mean, fine, you're afraid. But to just run away? And he's angry, Chloe. Like, really, really angry. I shouldn't have said anything about borrowing the pass. I'm sorry to have dragged you into this."

Chloe tightened her hold, offering what comfort she could. "Don't worry about that. We'll deal with Ted tomorrow. But for now, how are you feeling?"

"Like my heart is being torn apart… again," Penny admitted, the tears finally spilling over. "I'm so mad at him, but I'm also still very much in love with him. It's a horrible situation. I need to let him go, though. At this point, he's been more than clear about what he wants… and it's not me."

The words hung in the air between them, a painful truth that neither could deny. Penny knew that no matter how much it hurt, she had to move on. Nathan had made his choice, and now, she would have to make hers.

After Penny dropped Chloe off at the radio station, she drove through the city streets in silence. The neon lights blurred past, a dizzying wash of colors against the dark sky. The weight of the day pressed down on her, and every breath felt shallow, like she couldn't quite fill her lungs. She barely noticed when she pulled up to her favorite takeout spot, the one she always turned to when she needed something, anything, to fill the emptiness inside.

She ordered on autopilot, barely hearing her own voice as she listed off enough food for three people. By the time she made it home with the bags in hand, the smell of fried food and melted cheese was heavy in the air. Penny hadn't even realized how much she'd ordered until she saw the greasy spread on her coffee table. It was a familiar chaos—burgers, fries, chicken tenders, mozzarella sticks, and a couple of desserts to top it all off. Comfort food, for when the comfort felt out of reach.

She glanced at her phone, seeing missed texts from Mark and Stacie, but the thought of explaining the mess she'd just waded through made her stomach twist. She let the phone slip from her fingers onto the couch, sighing as she sank back into the cushions. The scene with Nathan replayed in her mind, his cold stare, his harsh words. The mention of more legal documents left a bitter taste in her mouth. Had she crossed a line she didn't even know existed? Was she now a character in some legal thriller, her life tangled up in invisible boundaries and unseen rules?

Pushing the thoughts away, she changed into a pair of old pajama bottoms and her favorite oversized sweatshirt. She wrapped herself in a worn quilt and settled into her usual spot on the couch. With the remote in hand, she began flicking through channels, stopping on a reality show where the drama was staged, predictable, and so far removed from her own chaotic reality that it felt like a temporary escape.

The steamer trunk that served as her coffee table was now

covered with takeout containers—a mountain of fried comfort piled high. Penny stared at the spread, almost amused at the cliché of it all. She was a hot mess—a walking stereotype of a woman drowning her sorrows in a sea of junk food. But tonight, she didn't care. Tonight, it was just her. Alone, with her comfort food, her thoughts, and the terrible reality show playing on the TV.

The hours drifted by in a haze. She didn't really taste the food as she ate, mechanically reaching for another bite, then another. By the time she had polished off everything, including the cookie dough she found stashed in the back of her freezer, she felt sick. Not just from the food, but from the realization that she was unsuccessfully trying to fill a void that food couldn't touch. The emptiness still gnawed at her, even as she pushed the empty containers away, her stomach full but her heart just as empty.

Finally, exhausted and numb, Penny dragged herself to bed. But sleep wouldn't come. She tossed and turned, the night pressing down like a weight on her chest. She reached for a notebook on her bedside table, flipping it open to a blank page. Her hand hovered over the paper, and then she began to write, pouring out everything she had been carrying inside. Every word felt like a release, each sentence a small act of letting go.

She wrote until her hand cramped, the words blurring together as her tears finally ran dry. The room was silent; the only sound was the quiet scratch of her pen against the page. When she finally set the notebook aside, she closed her eyes and prayed for sleep, a deep, dreamless sleep that would offer some relief. But as the hours dragged on, the darkness remained restless, haunted by the fragmented images of what could have been.

KEL SUMMERS

CHAPTER FIVE

Morning came too soon, and Penny awoke with the heavy realization that nothing had changed. She was still stuck in the same spiral, but today, she didn't have the energy to pretend otherwise. She pulled her hair into a messy bun, not caring about the stray strands that refused to cooperate. She grabbed the first pair of leggings she could find draped over her rocking chair and threw on a wrinkled t-shirt with a flannel over it, not even glancing in the mirror.

As Penny pulled into the parking lot, she immediately noticed Chloe pacing back and forth in front of the station. The sight sent a ripple of unease through her. Checking the time, Penny saw she had at least fifteen minutes before her show prep started. Yet, Chloe's anxious strides told her something was off.

The moment Chloe spotted her, she quickened her pace, practically jogging to meet Penny as she rounded the corner. Chloe's face was drawn, her expression tight with concern.

"What's wrong? I'm on time. Did something happen?" Penny asked, worry lacing her words. Her heart began to race, a sense of foreboding tightening her chest.

Chloe's eyes darted around nervously before settling back

on Penny. "All I know is Ted's been pacing his office, and he keeps asking if you're here yet. He looks upset, Penny. I'm guessing he found out about us trying to talk to Nathan yesterday. I still don't get why it's such a big deal, but he wants to see you right away. They've even queued up a repeat session for the show."

Penny felt a lump form in her throat. A repeat session? That meant Ted wanted to keep her off the air, which could only mean one thing—she was in trouble... big trouble. She glanced at Chloe, who looked just as rattled as she felt. The urge to turn around, to run, clawed at her, but she knew there was no escape from this. She had to face it.

Taking a steadying breath, Penny pushed through the front door and into the workroom, where Ted's voice immediately cut through the air, sharp and unyielding. "Penny! Get in here. Now!"

His growl cut through the room like a whip, and Penny froze. Her pulse quickened, and she could feel the weight of everyone's eyes on her as she moved toward Ted, who was standing in his office doorway. Ted's glare shifted briefly to Chloe, a silent reprimand for her attempt to warn Penny. Guilt written all over her face, she gave him an apologetic shrug before he disappeared into his office. Chloe had done what she could to warn Penny, but they both knew it wouldn't change what was about to happen.

Penny's thoughts spiraled, each one more frantic than the last. She forced herself to take a few deep breaths and hoped this wouldn't be as bad as she feared. But the pounding headache that suddenly struck her told her she was dead wrong. Every step felt heavier, dragging her closer to a confrontation she wasn't sure she was prepared for. As she approached Ted's office, she braced herself, dreading whatever awaited her on the other side of that door.

As Penny stepped into Ted's office, the air felt thick, like it was charged with the weight of unspoken accusations. Ted sat behind his desk, casually leaning back in his chair. Anyone walking by would think they were having a friendly chat. However, his furrowed eyebrows and the vein angrily pulsating in his forehead indicated to Penny that this conversation was going to be anything but friendly.

"Penny," Ted's voice was cold, cutting through the silence the moment she stepped inside. He didn't bother with pleasantries. "Did you happen to borrow the airport press pass from my drawer yesterday?"

Penny felt her heart drop. She swallowed, trying to keep her voice steady. "Yes, I…," she began, but Ted cut her off, his gaze sharp.

"And did you happen to follow Nathan to the airport using that pass?"

She looked down, unable to meet his eyes. The truth was already out there; denying it would only make things worse. "I think you know the answer to that," she replied softly.

Ted's eyes narrowed, and his voice became quieter, more measured, which, Penny realized, was more unnerving than if he were shouting at her. "We received a notice from Nathan's attorney yesterday that essentially cut all ties with the radio station. The radio station and its employees are expected to have nothing else to do with Nathan. The pass you used, which belongs to the radio station, and you being an employee of the radio station, gives Nathan reason to file a complaint against the station and possibly even take us to court."

Penny barely caught herself from rolling her eyes, muttering under her breath, "You've got to be kidding."

In an instant, Ted was on his feet, his hands pressing down on his desk with enough force to make it slide forward slightly. The action made Penny flinch, and her heart pounded harder in her chest. He straightened, his gaze bearing down on her, and spoke in a low, almost growling tone. "Do I look like I'm kidding, Penny?"

Penny's heart sank into her stomach. The gravity of the situation pressed down on her, making it hard to breathe. "Ted, I'm sorry. I didn't think about it when I took the pass. I just... well, I wasn't thinking."

Ted sighed heavily, the frustration etched in every line of his face. "Penny, I know you didn't mean for this to happen. But you've put us all in a tight spot. Nathan's given us an ultimatum. He'll let this go if we take *A Penny for Your Thoughts* off the air and... let you go. I can try to fight it, but even Ruth is angry. She doesn't like to be embarrassed, and you embarrassed her yesterday. I'm sorry, Penny."

Penny felt as if she'd been punched in the gut. Fired? Her job and the radio show were everything to her, and she'd just thrown it all away over one reckless decision. "Ted, please. Can't I talk to Ruth? Nathan's being unreasonable. I can agree never to contact him again—I'll delete his number, block him, whatever it takes. But I can't lose my job and the radio show because of this. This job, the show—it's my life."

Ted rubbed his forehead, looking as worn down as she felt. "I'm not sure that there is much I can do here. Letting you go isn't what I want either. But we need Ruth on our side, and as of last night, she most definitely is not. We're airing a repeat today so there will be no involvement from you. I'll talk to Ruth and do my best. But you cannot, under any circumstances, contact Nathan again."

With a weary swing of his hands, Ted motioned toward the door, the gesture was a silent command for her to leave. Penny didn't need any further prompting. She turned on her heel, her legs feeling like lead as she walked out, pulling the door closed behind her with a soft click.

When she stepped out into the hallway, she spotted Chloe and Walter waiting for her. By the look on their faces, Penny could only assume that they heard everything. She felt the sting of tears behind her eyes and blinked several times as she walked toward them.

"I still have everything I need to make that sniveling little weasel's world come crashing down," Walter muttered with a glint in his eye. His tone was only half-joking. "You just say the word. No one will ever know it came from you."

Penny managed a small laugh, shaking her head. Despite the storm of emotions swirling inside her, Walter's defiance was almost comforting. "Tempting as that is, I think I'll have to pass.

At least for now."

Chloe placed a reassuring hand on Penny's arm, her eyes soft with regret. "I'm so sorry, Penny. I shouldn't have encouraged you yesterday. I never thought it would lead to all this."

Penny pulled them both into a quick hug, drawing strength from their support. "Don't blame yourself, Chloe. This was my choice. I went after Nathan, not you. I just didn't expect... well, any of this."

They lingered for a moment, each of them absorbing the weight of what had just happened. Through the glass window, Penny caught a glimpse of Jake in the booth, keeping an eye on the clock while sneaking glances in their direction. She managed a tight-lipped smile and grabbed a bottle of water from the fridge, hoping the coolness would settle her nerves.

A minute later, Jake joined them, almost relieved to escape the booth. "Sorry. I would have come out sooner, but I had to keep things rolling in there." He paused, taking in their solemn faces. "You're still here, though. That's something, right? By the way," Jake leaned in closer to Penny. "I've got connections in Seattle. Just say the word, and we'll make Nathan regret he ever messed with you." He whispered, joining Walter in his attempt to lighten the mood.

Penny raised her hands, urging them to take a step back from planning Nathan's untimely demise. "Alright, let's not go full-on vigilante just yet. Besides, it's my fault. I shouldn't have taken the pass. And I shouldn't have told Nathan about it. All it did was give him ammunition. But right now, I have to focus on fixing things here. I'm more worried about convincing Ruth that I'm not a liability. I look like a crazed stalker, which… yeah, I suppose is valid. But I've got to make Ruth understand this isn't who I am."

The three of them started talking all at once, offering advice and solutions, each one trying to talk over the others. Jake darted back into the booth every now and then to keep the show on track, while Walter's calm and steady voice cut through the noise.

"You might think this sounds crazy," he said, meeting Penny's gaze. "But I think you should lean into the whole love angle. As much as I think Nathan is an idiot, I also think the two of you had something real. It seemed so natural. That might be why I'm so mad at him. There are so many people out there that want what you two had, and he was blind to it."

"Or he does realize it," Jake added, rejoining the conversation. "And like Ted said, he's scared to death."

Penny's mind whirred as she considered their words. *Could they be right? Did Nathan know exactly what he was throwing away? Was that what all of this was really about?*

Chloe's voice cut through her thoughts, soft but steady. "All of that may be true, but Nathan didn't show any sign of that last night. He was… brutal. I know it was hard to hear, Penny. Sorry."

Penny sighed, the fight slowly draining out of her. "Here's the thing," she began, her voice tentative but growing stronger as she spoke. "I do think Nathan loved me—or even still loves me. And I know that sounds crazy, especially after last night, but there's this whole 'thou doth protest too much' thing going on. It doesn't matter, though, because, for whatever reason, he's not willing to go there. That much is obvious."

Walter wasn't ready to give up just yet. "But that's what you need to show Ruth—that this wasn't about some wild attempt at revenge or harassment.," he suggested, his tone gentle but insistent. "Admit you were out of control, not out of craziness, but out of love. And agree to temper your reactions and steer clear of him, no matter how much it hurts. Show her that this experience makes you a better journalist and broadcaster."

"And cross your fingers that she's a hopeless romantic… and in a good mood," Jake added with a nervous laugh.

Penny considered their advice, the pieces of a plan taking shape in her mind. It made sense. The best way out of this might simply be by telling the truth. While Jake headed back to the booth to finish the show, Penny, Chloe, and Walter sat down to hash out the details. With each idea, Penny felt a bit more grounded, a bit more like she had a fighting chance. They worked through various angles, honing a strategy that they hoped would appeal to Ruth.

Finally, with their plan set, Penny felt the first pangs of hunger, and her growling stomach reminded her that she hadn't eaten since the greasy takeout the night before. "I think I need to eat something before I pass out," she said with a half-smile, turning to Chloe. "Come on. I'll buy you a coffee. It's the least I can do for dragging you into this whole mess."

"Sure. Let's go," Chloe agreed, and as they stepped out into the cool air, she started to apologize again for her part in the whole mess. But Penny cut her off with a wave of her hand.

"This is a Nathan-free zone," she insisted, giving Chloe a

playful nudge. "And you did nothing wrong. I promise. We're good."

Chloe smiled. Her relief was evident. "Good, because I don't have a lot of close friends, and losing you would really suck." It was the perfect lighthearted comment needed to finally ease the remaining tension.

They picked up muffins for Jake and Walter on the way back, and as they walked, they talked about anything but Nathan. By the time they returned to the station, the weight of the situation was somehow feeling more manageable, and Penny was starting to feel more confident that she could convince Ruth that this was all just a crazy misunderstanding.

When they stepped inside, Ruth was already there, waiting for her. Penny's heart skipped a beat, but with a steadying breath, she prepared herself. It was time to put their plan to the test.

KEL SUMMERS

CHAPTER SIX

"Good morning, Penny, I see you're still here." Ruth's voice cut through the air, sharp and unforgiving. "I trust Ted informed you of the fall-out after you ambushed Nathan at the airport last night."

The word "ambushed" stung, but Penny kept her composure. She knew she had to tread carefully. "Yes, ma'am," she replied, forcing her voice to remain calm. "And I wanted to apologize. I understand my action may have caused some issues, but I'd like to chance to explain myself—if you'll allow me.

Ruth's expression was unreadable, a mask of stern professionalism. "I'm sure Ted told you my husband is ill. I don't have time for this nonsense, Penny. So, I hope whatever you have to say makes my trip here worth my while."

Without waiting for a response, Ruth turned on her heel and led the way to one of the private offices, the sound of her footsteps echoing sharply against the tile floor. Walter quickly took the muffins out of Penny's hands and whispered, "Good luck," as he handed her the notebook with her presentation. She clutched it like a lifeline, holding it tightly to her chest as if it could somehow anchor her in the storm she was about to face.

Inside, the small space felt suffocating. The walls were cluttered with awards and framed photos, but it was the weight of Ruth's disappointment that made the room feel like it was closing in. Penny could feel the sweat prickling at the base of her neck as she took a seat across from Ruth.

Ruth didn't waste any time. "I don't have a lot of patience for excuses, Penny. And I certainly don't have the time to coddle you. So, I hope you have a very compelling reason for why I shouldn't fire you on the spot."

The bluntness of Ruth's words hung in the air, heavy and cold. Penny's heart pounded, but she knew this was her only chance. She took a deep breath, willing her voice to stay steady. "I really enjoy working here, Ruth," she said, her grip tightening on the notebook. "I know I've made mistakes, but I'm willing to own up to them."

Ruth raised an eyebrow, her gaze piercing, but she said nothing, prompting Penny to continue. This was it—the moment she'd been preparing for all morning. She could feel the weight of Ruth's gaze on her, unyielding and expectant.

Penny set down her notebook with deliberate care, taking the moment to gather her courage. "Ruth, I know what I did was wrong," she began, her words carrying a quiet but earnest plea for understanding. "I truly am sorry about last night. I never intended to ambush Nathan or put the radio station in a bad light. I let my emotions get the better of me, and I acted impulsively. But it wasn't out of recklessness or disregard for the station's reputation. It was out of love."

Ruth's expression barely shifted, but there was a flicker of something—skepticism, perhaps. "Love?" she repeated, her tone sharp. "Penny, this is a business, not a soap opera. Your actions have consequences, and you could have put the station in a very precarious position."

"Yes, ma'am, I realize that," Penny replied in a soft voice. "But maybe to truly understand why I behaved the way I did I should start from the beginning."

Ruth leaned back in her seat, clasping her hands together. "Please do."

Penny's heart raced as she recalled the whirlwind of emotions she'd experienced over the past few months. "I fell in love with Nathan the minute I met him, without even realizing it," she admitted, her voice laced with a vulnerability she rarely allowed herself to show. "He challenged me, made me want to be a better person, and encouraged me to reach for my dreams. Everything felt so natural with him, and when he decided to leave, it... well, it devastated me."

Ruth's face softened slightly, though she remained silent, her eyes locked on Penny, waiting. The silence stretched between them, but instead of being oppressive, it felt like an invitation for Penny to continue.

"I've always been someone who needs to know the 'why' behind things. Penny continued, her fingers fidgeting in her lap. "I know not everyone is going to like me or want to spend time with me, but I like to understand why. Maybe it's a flaw... a control issue that doesn't normally get out of hand. But with Nathan..."

"With Nathan, it got out of hand," Ruth interjected.

Penny nodded, guilt flooding her chest. "Yes, it did. I wanted to understand, and in trying to get closure, I let my emotions drive me to make poor decisions. I know that now. I shouldn't have tried to see him again, especially using the station's resources. I know I put the station at risk, and I promise I won't contact him again or try to see him. Last night was hard. It still hurts to shut the door, but he's not in the same place as I am. I don't know if he ever will be, so I just need to let it go."

Ruth leaned forward slightly, her posture less rigid, her arms resting loosely on the table. "Can I ask you something?"

Penny braced herself, not sure what was coming next. "Of course."

Ruth's voice was softer now, curious. "What do you love most about him?"

Penny blinked, the question catching her off guard. She hadn't prepared for this—hadn't expected to have to articulate the very thing she'd been struggling to understand herself. She took a moment, letting the question sink in before she answered.

"I think…" Penny started, choosing her words carefully, "what I love most about him is how he made me feel like I could be more than I was. I was already confident, but he… challenged me in ways I didn't expect. He wasn't afraid to push back when I needed it, and he wasn't afraid to be vulnerable either. It was like we were constantly making each other better versions of ourselves."

She paused, glancing down at her hands, fingers tracing the edge of the notebook as if the tactile connection would ground her. "Nathan had this way of seeing the best in me when I couldn't see it in myself. That's rare, and it made me want to be the kind of person who could live up to his view of me. I didn't feel like I had to put on an act or pretend to be anything other than who I was with him. And maybe that's why it hurt so much when he left. Because it felt like he was walking away from everything I thought I was becoming. And I didn't understand how he could let that go so easily."

Ruth was silent for a moment, her gaze softening as she studied Penny. "That's a complicated place to be, Penny. But you need to understand something—Nathan's journey is his own. Just because he walked away doesn't mean you weren't enough. It just means he wasn't ready for what you had together."

Penny swallowed, her chest tight with emotion. "I think I understand that now," she whispered.

Ruth's slow nod was followed by a small, unexpected smile tugging at the corners of her mouth. "You know, Penny, you remind me of myself when I was younger," she said, her voice softer now, reflective. "Back when I was trying to convince William that I was exactly what he needed. He was just as stubborn as Nathan."

Penny blinked, watching as Ruth's eyes seemed to glaze over with memories. It was as if she'd been transported back to her own whirlwind romance, and for a moment, the sharp edges of her professional exterior softened.

"You know Nathan was engaged once," Ruth continued, her voice quieter, more intimate. "Did he ever mention that?"

Penny nodded, a dull ache rising in her chest. "Yeah, he did." She hesitated, then added, "He also told Ted he was afraid he was falling too hard for me, that he didn't want to get hurt again. Ted shared that with me, and... I'm not sure it was helpful. It made me feel like there was hope, which may have led to my poor judgment last night."

Ruth's eyes narrowed, considering Penny's words. She tapped her fingers lightly on the table, her gaze fixed on something distant, as if she were weighing her next move carefully. Then, with a resigned sigh, she leaned back in her chair. "I don't think you need to be fired, Penny. I just think you're in love. And I may regret saying this, but... I think you should try once more."

Penny's mouth fell open in shock. She stared at Ruth, trying to process what she'd just heard. "Try again?" she echoed, disbelief coloring her voice. "Ruth, you can't be serious. Not even twenty-four hours ago, you told Ted to fire me because I ambushed Nathan. Now you're telling me I should try again?"

Ruth's calm expression didn't waver, though a hint of amusement flickered in her eyes. "I know it sounds contradictory, but love isn't always logical, Penny. Sometimes, when it comes to matters of the heart, things aren't as black and white as we'd like them to be." She paused, studying Penny with a look of quiet intensity before continuing.

"Love... love has a way of making us do crazy things. And

sometimes, those things lead us to where we're supposed to be. I see something in you, Penny—a determination and a passion. And I think you owe it to yourself to take one last chance and see where that leads. Besides, Nathan doesn't realize what he's doing. I fully believe he's just as in love with you as you are with him. But you scare him."

Penny sat there, stunned. Ruth, who just fifteen minutes ago had been a wall of icy professionalism, was now speaking to Penny like a mentor, maybe even a friend. "Ruth, I... I don't know what to say," Penny stammered, her emotions threatening to spill over.

"Don't say anything," Ruth replied, a soft smile playing on her lips. "Just think about it. And if you decide to try again, do it with everything you've got. No half-measures, Penny. If you're going to fight for something, fight with your whole heart, or not at all."

Penny nodded slowly. Her mind was racing as she tried to process everything. She had walked into this room expecting the worst, but instead, she had been given something she had given up on—another chance.

Penny's voice wavered as she looked at Ruth, her eyes searching for answers that seemed just out of reach. "How do I fix this? Surely, you're not suggesting that I ambush him again."

Ruth studied her, a glimmer of calculation behind her eyes. "No," she said firmly. "Leave that to me."

Penny's brow furrowed, confused. "You?"

Ruth nodded, her expression thoughtful. "I know I'm playing both sides here. I want to see Nathan with the woman he should be with—you—but I also need to keep the peace between the newspaper and the station. That's my job. I reacted too quickly last night when I told Ted to fire you, and for that, I apologize. I let my frustration get the best of me after hearing only Nathan's side of the story. Now that I've heard you out, I understand that his actions were completely fueled by his own fears. He is so much like his father, my brother. He could never see the forest for the trees, either."

Ruth patted her hands on the table. There was a finality in the gesture, as if she had come to a decision. She pushed back her chair with a soft scrape against the floor and stood, giving Penny one last and lingering look.

"And Penny?" she said, her voice softer now yet still carrying the weight of everything unsaid.

Penny turned to face her, meeting Ruth's steady gaze. "Yes, ma'am."

"Don't make me regret this."

Penny swallowed, feeling the pressure of Ruth's words settle on her shoulders. She nodded, unable to say much more as Ruth turned and left the room. The click of the door closing behind her echoed in the sudden silence, leaving Penny alone with her thoughts.

The quiet felt deafening now, the intensity of the conversation still hanging in the air. Penny sat there for a moment, staring at the door Ruth had just walked through, replaying her words in her mind. Ruth's sudden shift from adversary to ally had caught her off guard, leaving her feeling like she was standing on unfamiliar ground. How Ruth planned to pull this off was beyond Penny's comprehension, and the thought of how Nathan might react left her stomach in knots.

But then, a single thought broke through the fog of uncertainty. She was being given another chance—not just with her job, but maybe, just maybe, with Nathan too. The realization hit her like a splash of cold water, refreshing and invigorating. And in that instant, Penny realized that this wasn't just about Nathan anymore. It was about her and about what she was willing to fight for.

KEL SUMMERS

CHAPTER SEVEN

Feeling lighter than she had in days, Penny pushed away from the table, her chair sliding across the floor with a quiet sigh. She stood, a renewed sense of purpose settling over her as she headed back to her desk, where Chloe and the others were anxiously waiting for her.

"What happened? We were about ready to come get you," Chloe said, jumping to her feet when she spotted Penny. "We didn't hear any yelling, so that has to be good, right?"

Penny shook her head, still trying to process her conversation with Ruth, as she let out a long breath. "Well, I'm not getting fired, and I don't think I will be anytime soon, either. For that, I am grateful, because I love you guys, and I can't imagine not working with you."

The words tumbled out with more emotion than she had expected, catching even her by surprise. She glanced at her desk, where a single muffin sat waiting. "I'm starving," she said, grabbing the muffin as she dropped down in her desk chair.

"You're always starving," Jake said, rolling his eyes. But Chloe gave her a triumphant grin. "I almost had to fist fight these guys to leave you that muffin. So, you're welcome."

Penny laughed. "Well, I love you just a little more than them right now," she teased, tearing off a piece of the muffin and popping it in her mouth.

"Okay, okay. Let's not get off track here," Walter said, not willing to let the conversation get sidetracked. "It's great that you get to keep your job, but she didn't say anything else? You two gals were in there forever."

Still trying to wrap her mind around what Ruth had said, Penny chewed slowly, buying herself a few more seconds before answering. "Okay, here's where it get's weird, but I don't even care. I told Ruth everything we talked about—how I'd fallen in love with Nathan without even realizing it, how devastated I was when he left so suddenly, and how that led to some bad choices. I even promised to never contact him again."

"And she agreed?" Jake asked, leaning in slightly, his curiosity now fully engaged. "I mean, I'm assuming she did since, again, you're still here."

Penny paused, the memory of Ruth's surprising advice lingering in her mind. "Yes and no." she said, her voice filled with uncertainty. "She agreed that I had made some bad choices, but she didn't agree to me never contacting him again. She wants me to try again with him."

The room was silent for a beat, the words hanging in the air as her friends exchanged confused looks.

"Nope. No way. Absolutely not!" They all jumped, at the sound of Ted's voice behind them. "What is she thinking? You and Chloe both said he was crystal clear yesterday. And I don't want to take another late-night phone call from her ranting and raving about how this whole mess is blowing up in our faces. She wanted you fired, and now she wants you to try again?"

Penny shrugged, still trying to wrap her mind around it herself. "Exactly! I don't get it either. But she told me not to worry about it, and that she'd handle things. Honestly, I'm just relieved that I didn't lose my job. Right now, that's all I care about."

Chloe raised her water bottle in a mock toast. "Here's to that! The gang is staying together."

Ted looked at them as if they were all crazy. He eyes darted from Walter to Jake, then Chloe, and back to Penny before his shoulders slumped in silent resignation. "I guess you're right. We're not losing Penny, and that's worth celebrating."

The group cheered in mock celebration, garnering curious looks from some of the other on-air personalities and support staff working close by who had no idea of the drama that had been unfolding around them.

"Alright, alright," Jake said, bringing the conversation back to business. "Now that the crisis has been averted, let's talk about the plan for next week's show. We are making headway with the new format, but I want to hit the ground running next week and really bring it home."

The team gathered around Penny's desk, their focus shifting from Penny's drama to the show. Chloe's marketing ideas sparked a lively discussion, and soon, the next few weeks of content began to take shape with surprising ease. As Penny listened to the brainstorming around her, she felt a sense of peace settle over her. It wasn't about the future or what might happen next—it was about this moment, and for now, that was enough.

As the meeting wrapped up, Walter leaned in close, his voice low and sincere. "Seriously, I'm glad you're sticking around. This place wouldn't be the same without you."

"Thanks, Walter. Have a good night."

"You, too, Penny," Walter responded before turning to leave.

Penny's heart swelled with love as she watched his retreating figure for a moment, before turning to Chloe. "Hey, do you have plans later? I am thinking Happy Hour at Franco's. I can invite Mark and Stacie. I have to fill them in on everything that's happened, and they've been dying to meet you."

Chloe's face lit up. "I'm free! I would love to finally meet them. I feel like we've been trying to make this happen forever."

"Great! I'll text them now."

Penny stood in the hallway, her phone in hand, her fingers hovering over the screen as she typed a quick message to Mark and Stacie.

> **Penny:** *Crazy day! Need to fill you in. Meet for happy hour at Franco's? Chloe's coming, too.*

The thought of her three best friends finally meeting felt like the perfect end to a day that had started so disastrously. It was as if the universe was finally throwing her a bone, and she was ready to take it.

After sending the text, she dropped her phone on her desk

and darted into the bathroom, her steps light with anticipation. When she flicked on the light, the harsh fluorescent bulbs illuminated her reflection, and Penny braced herself for what she'd see. The face staring back at her was tired, yes, but not as defeated as she had feared. Her hair was a bit of a mess, her eyes slightly puffy from the stress of the day, but there was also a spark of determination in her eyes that hadn't been there earlier. Still, she decided a shower was non-negotiable before heading to happy hour.

As she washed and dried her hands, she glanced at herself one more time in the mirror before leaving the bathroom.

"Chloe, I look like a complete wreck today. I can't believe you didn't say anything. It's no wonder I can't keep…"

"Penny." Chloe's voice was quiet but urgent, cutting her off mid-sentence.

Penny frowned, turning to face her. "What? Sorry, did you say something?"

"Penny," Chloe repeated, her voice a little louder now, her expression unreadable. "Nathan's here."

CHAPTER EIGHT

Chloe's words didn't register at first, and when they did, Penny let out a laugh, her mind instantly flashing back to the day Nathan had shown up out of the blue to declare his love for her. Why Chloe thought this was a good joke was beyond her, but she played along, her eyes still on her phone. "Right. Not funny, Chloe. Did Mark and Stacie reply yet?" she asked, her fingers poised to type.

But when she finally looked up, the expression on Chloe's face stopped her cold. The serious, almost anxious set of Chloe's mouth, the way her eyes flickered toward the right—something about it made Penny's heart skip a beat. Slowly, she turned her head, and her breath caught in her throat.

There he was—Nathan—standing in the doorway.

For a moment, everything else seemed to fade away. The noise of the office, the buzz of fluorescent lights, even the faint hum of a distant conversation—all of it was drowned out by the sight of Nathan. He looked both familiar and foreign at the same time, standing there with his broad shoulders and dark wavy hair just as she remembered and that drop-dead gorgeous smile she had fallen for. But it was those piercing blue eyes that always seemed to see right through her, that locked on hers and took her breath away.

It infuriated her that, even now, even after everything, he still had this kind of power over her. But she wasn't going to let him know that. Not after everything he'd put her through. So, she swallowed hard, squared her shoulders, and walked toward him with her chin held high.

"Nathan." Her voice was steady, but there was an underlying tension she couldn't quite shake. "What are you doing here? Did Ruth ask you to come?"

Nathan stepped forward, his smile fading into something more serious, something that mirrored the vulnerability in his eyes. "Ruth?" He seemed momentarily thrown. "No. She left me a message, but I haven't called her back yet. As soon as I landed, I came straight here." He paused, running a hand through his hair. "I haven't been able to stop thinking about how I acted. About how stupid I've been. Not just last night, but… for the past few weeks."

He stopped, his words hanging in the air, and Penny could see the conflict in his eyes. There was hesitation there, a mirror of her own uncertainty, and she could tell he was struggling to find the right thing to say.

"Nathan," she said, her voice softer now, but still laced with frustration. "Why are you really here?"

He took another step toward her, his gaze never leaving hers. "Penny, I've really messed things up," he admitted, his voice raw. "I came here to talk to Ted, and to tell him I was wrong to demand he fire you. That was… that was me being scared and acting like an idiot." He shook his head, as if disgusted with himself. "But when I saw you were still here, I knew I couldn't leave without talking to you, too."

Penny stood there, arms crossed, feeling a swirl of emotions—relief, anger, and something else... she wasn't sure what it was. She had wanted an apology, had needed it. But now that it was here, it didn't feel as satisfying as she'd thought it would. It just made everything more... complicated.

"I don't know what you want me to say, Nathan." Her voice wavered, the anger she had been clinging to slipping away, leaving her exposed. "You can't keep doing this... I can't keep doing this."

Nathan closed the distance between them, his eyes filled with a desperation she wasn't used to seeing. "Penny, I love you," he said, the words tumbling out like a confession. "The first time I saw you, I knew you were different. And from the minute I met you, I've loved you. I know I hurt you, Penny... more than once. I was scared. I didn't know how to handle what I was feeling, and I pushed you away when I should have fought to keep you."

He reached for her hand, but she stepped back, her eyes searching his, trying to make sense of everything.

"I don't know if I can trust you, Nathan," she said, her voice breaking just slightly. "You left. Twice. You shut me out when all I wanted was to be there for you."

"I know," Nathan whispered, his voice thick with regret. "I was an idiot. I'm not asking you to forgive me right now. I just... I need to know if you'd give me another chance. A second—well, a third—chance to make this right."

Penny's heart pounded in her chest, her mind spinning. This was the moment she had longed for, the moment she had imagined so many times in the quiet of her living room, when the ache of his absence felt unbearable. And yet, standing here now, hearing those words from him... it wasn't as simple as she thought it would be.

She glanced over at Chloe, who stood frozen near her desk, watching the scene unfold with wide eyes. It was only then that Penny realized the office had gone strangely quiet, and she knew the others were probably listening too. But none of that mattered in this moment. Right now, it was just her and Nathan, standing on the precipice of something she wasn't sure she was ready for.

"I don't know, Nathan," Penny finally said, her voice barely above a whisper. "I don't know if I can go through this again."

Nathan took a deep breath, his hands at his sides, his eyes pleading. "I know it's a lot to ask. But if there's even a part of you that still feels what I feel, please... let me prove it to you."

Penny stared at him, the words swirling around her, tugging at her heart, and she had no idea what the right answer was. He was here, standing in front of her, asking for another chance. And despite everything, despite the hurt and the anger, part of her... a big part of her... wanted to say yes.

The question was, could she?

CHAPTER NINE

"Please say something."

Nathan's voice, raw and pleading, hung in the air between them.

Penny stood frozen, her hands trembling despite her efforts to clench them into fists, willing herself to stay steady. She could feel the eyes of everyone in the room on her, the weight of their silent anticipation pressing down on her as if they were all waiting… waiting for her to decide how the next scene in this emotional drama would play out.

But how could she give them what they were waiting for, when she didn't even know herself?

Her gaze dropped to the floor, the weight of his words pressing down on her. She'd been on this exhausting roller coaster for months, and the constant ups and downs had worn her thin. It was enough to drive anyone mad, and frankly, Penny wasn't sure how much of her sanity remained intact. Nathan had that effect on her—he always had. But despite everything, despite the hurt and confusion, this was what she had wanted, right? Another chance? And now, here he was, standing in front of her, asking for just that.

But Penny felt no joy in the moment. She only felt the sharp sting of uncertainty.

"Nathan," she began, her voice soft but steady, "your reactions... they've been tearing me apart." She lifted her eyes to meet his, her heart aching at the vulnerability written across his face. "One minute, you're telling me you can't live without me, and the next, you're on a plane, flying across the country, acting like I never mattered. And then...," her voice cracked, her emotions bubbling up despite her attempts to hold them back. "You tried to get me fired."

The words felt heavy as they left her lips, each one carrying the weight of her frustration, her hurt. She shook her head, her voice gaining strength as she continued. "Men say women are the emotionally charged ones, but you—you have me beat, Nathan. I'm really at a loss here. I don't mean to sound cruel, but I'm just... I'm exhausted."

She could see the redness creeping into Nathan's face, the way his jaw tightened. He looked like he had been struck by her words, and maybe he had. Penny had spent so long letting his actions get under her skin that she couldn't help but feel a grim satisfaction in watching her words hit home. But despite the anger simmering in her, she could see something else in his eyes—something that made everything harder. Was it regret, maybe even shame?

Nathan took a small, hesitant step forward. "You're right. You're absolutely right," he said, his voice quiet, as though he was admitting something to himself as much as to her. He exhaled sharply, as if releasing a weight he had been carrying for too long.

"I've been a jerk. A complete idiot. And I know I've hurt you, Penny, in ways that I can't take back." His voice wavered, and for the first time, she saw a crack in the defenses he'd always kept up. "Your friends probably hate me by now, and I wouldn't blame them if they did. I wouldn't blame you if you hated me, too. But I need you to know I never meant to hurt you. I was just... scared. And I know that's not an excuse."

Penny's heart twisted. Despite everything, she couldn't deny the pang of empathy she felt for him at that moment. Hearing him admit his fears, seeing him like this—vulnerable, raw—it was hard not to feel something. But apologies didn't erase what had been done. They didn't magically rebuild trust overnight. And the reality was that Nathan had broken her trust more than once.

She drew in a slow breath, weighing her next words carefully. "I still love you, Nathan. If I didn't, I wouldn't have gone chasing after you last night like some love-struck fool. I wouldn't have humiliated myself by trying to make sense of this whole mess." She shook her head, the weight of everything they had been through pressing down on her chest. "But I can't keep doing this. I can't keep feeling like you've got one foot out the door, waiting for the moment to run."

Nathan winced as her words sank in. His eyes were bright with unshed tears, his voice barely above a whisper when he spoke again. "I know. I know things have to change." He took another step closer, raising his hands as if in surrender, his voice trembling with emotion. "I'll do whatever it takes to fix this, Penny. I'll work every day to rebuild the trust I've broken, no matter how long it takes. But please... I'm asking for one more chance. One more."

Penny stared at him, the man she had once been so sure of, now standing in front of her asking for a do-over. Her mind raced, searching for some kind of clarity in the haze of emotions. She had wanted him to come back, had wanted to hear him say those words. But now, in the thick of it, it wasn't as simple as she had thought it would be.

She wanted to believe him. She wanted to believe that this time would be different, that he had truly changed, and that they could make this work. But the scars of the past were still fresh, and they couldn't be smoothed over with promises and apologies.

Silence settled between them, thick and suffocating. Penny could feel the weight of every eye in the room, but she no longer cared. This wasn't about them—this was about her and Nathan, and whether or not she believed he could change or would change.

She studied his face, searching for any sign that this time might be different. That this time, he wouldn't leave her standing alone in the wreckage of their relationship. His eyes held hers, raw and open, and it was the first time in a long while that she saw no walls, no barriers between them.

"I think..." she started, her voice measured. "I think we need to talk. Really talk. Longer than just this." She paused, her words hanging in the air, the weight of them pressing down on both of them. "If you're serious about trying again, we need to figure out what that looks like. No more grand gestures or promises that fizzle out. I need time, and I need honesty. Can you give me that?"

Nathan nodded, the tension in his shoulders easing slightly, relief washing over his face like a wave. "I can. I will," he said, his voice filled with conviction. "I owe you that much, at the very least."

Penny exhaled, and a small sense of clarity finally broke through the fog. "I'm going home now," she said, her words measured. "I don't know what my answer will be, but we can start by talking, really talking. If you're willing to do that, then you can meet me there."

Nathan's expression softened, his eyes brightening with something that almost resembled hope. A small smile crept onto his face. "I'll be there," he promised. His voice was quiet but certain. "And Penny... thank you."

Without another word, he turned and walked toward the door, his movements careful, almost cautious. He avoided the wide-eyed stares of the others in the room, making a silent exit. The soft click of the door closing behind him seemed to release the collective breath everyone had been holding and the room erupted into a flurry of voices.

"What the hell just happened?" Walter blurted, his eyes wide with shock.

"I can't believe he just showed up here like that," Jake muttered, shaking his head in disbelief. "The nerve of that guy..."

Chloe, still standing near the door, looked like she couldn't decide whether to be relieved or concerned. "Are you okay?" she asked, rushing to Penny's side. "I mean, that was... a lot. Are you really thinking about taking him back?"

Penny sank into her chair, her legs suddenly feeling like they could no longer hold her up. She pressed her palms against her face, taking a deep breath before answering. "I don't know," she admitted, her voice muffled through her hands. "I don't know what I'm going to do."

Jake leaned against the edge of her desk, crossing his arms as he studied her. "So… you're really going to meet with him? After everything?"

Penny dropped her hands and looked up, the exhaustion of the past few months etched into her features. "I don't know what else to do, Jake," she said softly. "I can't just… not try. I still love him."

The room quieted a bit at her admission, the weight of her words sinking in. They all knew how much Nathan had hurt her, how much she had struggled to keep herself together after he walked away the last time. But love wasn't something that could be neatly boxed away, and no one in the room could pretend otherwise.

On the other hand, she felt a little like the girl who cried wolf. If she took him back and he broke her heart again…, when would they stop supporting her? At some point, doesn't it become her own fault for falling for it all over again?

Chloe knelt beside her chair, her eyes filled with sympathy. "Just promise me you'll protect yourself this time," she said, her voice barely above a whisper. "I don't want to see you go through that kind of pain again."

Penny managed a small, tired smile. "I'll try," she said softly, though even she knew there were no guarantees.

Ted, who had remained silent through the whole exchange, finally spoke up, his tone uncharacteristically gentle. "Just... don't let him walk all over you, Penny. You deserve better than that."

She nodded, though deep down, she wasn't sure what she deserved anymore. All she knew was that she couldn't ignore the part of her that still believed in the possibility of something more. Something better, maybe. Or maybe she was setting herself up for the same heartbreak all over again.

The truth of the matter was that she thought he might really be the one for her. It was the whole reason she'd tried so desperately to hold on. Even when he moved across the country. Even when he tried to get her fired. From the outside looking in, she knew it looked like she was just a glutton for punishment. But there was so much more to it than that. It wasn't something she could explain. One would just have to be in her shoes to truly understand.

"Thank you, guys. I don't know what I'm going to do," she quietly admitted. "I know it's crazy to give him another chance, but my gut tells me not to give up on him. Not yet. I won't blame any of you if you want off this ride, but..." She trailed off, feeling the weight of the decision looming ahead of her.

Chloe reached out and squeezed Penny's hand. "I don't know what I would do in your position. I know what I think I would do...which is tell him to go fly a kite. But when it came down to it, I can't promise you I could follow through on that. This is your call, and whatever you decide, I will support you. Now, I'll be honest and say if he breaks your heart again, my support might include a little bit of attitude, but I'll still be here."

Penny laughed, the tension breaking for a brief moment. "Fair enough. I can live with that."

"I agree with Chloe. I don't like the guy, but that's mainly because I really like the guy. I'm sure that makes no sense. The two of you together just makes sense. I don't understand why he can't see that." Walter shrugged his shoulders and offered Penny a hug.

"Actually, that makes a lot of sense. Thanks, Walter."

Standing up, Penny grabbed her bag and slung it over her shoulder, casting a quick glance at her friends. "I'll see you all on Monday," she said, her voice steady but distant. "I'll let you know what happens."

As she walked out of the office, leaving behind the concerned murmurs and curious looks, Penny's heart was pounding out of sync with her mind. It was like her emotions were playing a tug-of-war. Her heart pulled her toward excitement that Nathan was back in town, waiting to talk. While at the same time, her mind was weighed down by exhaustion, unsure of what would happen next. The rollercoaster ride had been going on for so long, she wasn't sure how to get off, and she wasn't sure if her heart could take another dip.

CHAPTER TEN

As Penny slid into the driver's seat, her hand instinctively reached for her phone. She hovered over the screen, ready to text Mark and Stacie. But then, she hesitated. She knew what their reactions would be. They'd tell her she was crazy for even considering Nathan again, reminding her of all the pain he'd put her through. They had been her rocks during the worst of it, their unwavering support pulling her out of that deep pit of heartache. But right now? Did she really need their opinions? Or did she need to navigate this on her own for once?

Penny let out a sigh, her fingers hovering over the screen before she typed a quick message: *"Raincheck on happy hour. I'll explain later."* She hit send and dropped her phone into the cup holder. The silence in the car felt heavy as she stared out the windshield, the weight of the situation pressing down on her. She had no idea what was going to happen tonight.

Driving home, Penny's thoughts swirled like a storm as she imagined all the different ways the upcoming conversation might unfold. Was she strong enough to stand her ground this time? What if he said all the right things again, only to leave her feeling hollow weeks later? She bit her lip, thinking about her "cool" self—

the version of her that would have all the perfect comebacks, the one who wouldn't get hurt so easily. Too bad that version of her was likely lounging by an imaginary pool somewhere, laughing at how messy this had all become.

With each passing mile, she felt the knot of resolve tightening in her chest. She knew what she wanted to do, but that didn't make the fear any easier to shake. The fear of opening herself up only to be let down, again. The fear of being made a fool. She hated the sting of embarrassment, the taste of defeat. But maybe, just maybe, she was starting to care less about what others thought. This wasn't about them, after all. It was about her following her own heart and speaking her own truth, no matter how uncertain the path seemed.

The familiar curve of her street came into view and when she turned the corner and spotted Nathan's car parked out front, and her heart did a nervous little flip. *"Darn it,"* she mumbled. Why did her heart always betray her like this? For just a moment, she wished she didn't feel so much for him. It would make everything simpler. But she pushed that thought aside, exhaling slowly as she turned off the engine and reached for her bag in the back seat.

Nathan stepped off the porch as soon as he saw her, that familiar look of hesitation and regret clouding his eyes. He quickly crossed the short distance to her and reached to take her bag.

"I'm good, thank you. Just the one bag," she said, her voice polite but distant. She wasn't going to make this easy for him.

Nathan's hand fell awkwardly to his side, and for a moment,

he looked as though he wasn't sure what to do. "Thanks for agreeing to talk with me," he said softly. There was a hint of defeat in his voice, his words carrying the weight of his regret. "I know you could have easily said no."

Penny gave him a small, almost imperceptible nod. "Nothing about this is easy." She turned toward the door, fumbling with her keys before unlocking it. "Alexa, turn on the lights," she said as she stepped inside, the familiar warmth of her home enveloping her. But even within the safety of her own space, she could feel the tension of what was about to unfold.

"Sit wherever you want. I'm going to go change," she said, her tone even, giving him no room for conversation. She didn't wait for his response before heading to her bedroom, needing the brief escape.

Once she was behind the closed door, Penny leaned against it, exhaling deeply. The tension she'd been holding in began to release, but only slightly. Her fingers traced the edge of the dresser as she debated what to wear. Something comfortable. Something that didn't make her feel exposed. She changed into her favorite leggings and an oversized t-shirt, the soft fabric offering a small sense of calm.

As she stared at her reflection in the mirror, she thought about what would happen next and decided she wasn't going to rush this. She wanted Nathan to wait. *He needs to understand that everything doesn't happen on his terms.*

When Penny finally returned to the living room, she found Nathan sitting on the edge of the couch, his hands were clasped together as he stared at the floor. He looked up as she entered, and his eyes searched her face for an answer or at least a clue of what she was thinking.

Penny grabbed a pillow from the armchair and settled on the couch across from him, hugging it to her chest like a shield. She was fully aware of the barrier it created between them, but for now, it was a necessary buffer.

"Do you want to go first?" she asked. Her voice was softer than she intended, but steady. She watched as Nathan considered the question. She was sure, just like her, he'd been working out this conversation in his head already. After all, he was the one who asked to talk to her this time.

Nathan shifted in his seat, rubbing the back of his neck in that familiar way he always did when he was uncomfortable. Finally, his voice came out, quiet but deliberate. "I know… I know I've really messed things up. I don't expect you to just forgive me. But I meant what I said—I want to fix this, Penny. I want to be better."

Penny didn't say anything for a moment, letting the words hang in the air. She watched him carefully, measuring his sincerity, feeling the weight of all the hurt he had caused. It would've been easy to just let him in again, to let her heart take over, but she wasn't that same girl anymore. She couldn't be.

"What does 'better' look like to you, Nathan?" she finally asked, her voice calm but firm. "Because I don't want to keep playing this game where you come back just long enough to leave again. I deserve more than that."

Nathan's eyes softened, and he leaned forward, his elbows resting on his knees. "You're right. You deserve more than I've given you, and I'm sorry for all the times I made you feel like you didn't matter." His voice wavered slightly, and Penny could see the cracks in his facade. "I know I have a lot of work to do to prove that to you. But I'm willing to do it. I'm not here to make promises I can't keep. I'm here to ask you to give me a chance to show you that I've changed. That I *want* to change."

Penny hugged the pillow tighter, her eyes narrowing slightly. She had heard those words before. "Wanting to change is one thing, Nathan. But following through is another. I'm not looking for grand gestures or apologies. I'm looking for something real."

Her heart pounded. Each beat was filled with the weight of uncertainty. She knew she loved him—she'd never doubted that. But love alone hadn't been enough to prevent the mess they'd found themselves in. She quietly watched him, waiting for him to say more.

KEL SUMMERS

CHAPTER ELEVEN

Nathan shifted slightly, inhaling deeply as if bracing himself for what he was about to say. He finally looked up at her, his eyes full of remorse. "I think... I know I owe you an explanation. For a lot of things," he started, his voice low and raw. "I've acted like a complete lunatic pretty much since the night we met."

Penny raised an eyebrow, trying to lighten the heaviness in the room just a little. "Well, the night we met, you were actually on point. The crazy behavior started a couple of days after that."

Nathan chuckled softly, the sound full of self-deprecation, before his expression sobered. "That's fair," he admitted. "I know I told you about my ex-fiancé... but I don't think I ever told you how much our break-up really messed me up."

The confession lingered between them, fragile but honest. Penny stayed quiet, giving him the space to let the words come, not wanting to rush him.

"When she broke up with me," he continued, his voice cracking slightly, "I was blindsided. Even though, deep down, I knew she was right. We weren't good for each other, but that didn't make the rejection hurt any less." He paused, his eyes flicking up to meet Penny's before quickly looking away again, as if the admission was too much. "And after that, I started questioning everything. If I could be so wrong about us, about her, how could I trust myself to be right about anyone else? So, when I started falling for you... I panicked. I thought, if I left first, it wouldn't hurt as much. So, I jumped at the first opportunity."

The vulnerability in his voice was palpable, and Penny felt her heart twist. She knew that fear—she'd lived it, too. The fear of being wrong, of being hurt, of giving too much of yourself only to watch it crumble. She paused, trying to steady her emotions.

"I understand that," she said softly, her voice barely above a whisper. She shifted slightly, loosening her grip on the pillow. "I've been in your shoes. When Jeremy ended things, I was devastated. And realizing he was right, that we weren't meant to be, that stung even more. So, yeah, I get it."

Nathan's shoulders slumped, the weight of her words sinking in. He shifted on the couch, inching closer to her, his eyes filled with regret. "And now, I'm the one doing the hurting," he admitted. "I've done a hell of a job at it too. A+ student." He let out a bitter laugh. "I never wanted things to get this messed up. I just... I got scared, and I panicked."

Penny looked down at her hands, her fingers absentmindedly tracing the seams of the pillow in her lap. She understood his fear—she truly did. But understanding didn't make it easier to forgive, and it didn't make the hurt any less real.

"I get that," she said, her voice softer now. "But you can't keep doing this, Nathan. Sooner or later, I won't be able to recover.

No matter how much I might love you."

The words came out before she could stop them, the weight of her confession settling into the space between them. Penny hadn't planned on saying it out loud, hadn't planned on laying her heart so bare, but now that it was out there, she couldn't take it back.

Nathan's eyes widened slightly at her admission, and for a brief moment, he looked like he didn't know how to respond. But Penny didn't want to make a big deal out of it. She pressed on, her voice steady even as her emotions swirled inside her.

"At some point, I have to protect myself," she continued. "There are plenty of people who think I should've already hit that point by now." She paused, her gaze meeting his, the intensity of her emotions making her heart race. "But my gut… my gut tells me you're worth it. That we're worth it." She sighed, the weight of her next words settling heavily in her chest. "But, Nathan, when the warranty on that gut feeling runs out, I can't promise you'll get another chance. I'm not trying to threaten you. I just need you to know where I stand."

Nathan stared at her, his expression conflicted, torn between relief and the realization that her love wasn't unconditional. Not anymore.

For a moment, Penny worried she had pushed him too far, that her honesty might scare him away again. The room fell into a tense silence, the only sound the faint ticking of the clock on the wall. But then, slowly, Nathan moved closer, his hand reaching out to gently brush a strand of hair from her face.

Before she could fully process it, his lips were on hers, soft and urgent, filled with all the words he hadn't been able to say. Penny melted into the kiss, her heart racing as electricity surged through her body. It felt like coming home, like everything she had been waiting for had finally arrived.

When they finally pulled apart, breathless, Penny looked at him, her eyes wide with wonder. "Wow," she whispered, her voice shaky but filled with a quiet certainty. "There's no coming back from that. You're stuck with me now."

Nathan smiled, a slow, tender smile that reached his eyes as he pulled her closer, her head resting on his shoulder. "There's no other place I want to be," he murmured, his voice warm and filled with conviction. "You're perfect for me, Penny. I'm so glad I finally realized it. I'm going to spend every day proving it to you."

CHAPTER TWELVE

The blaring of the alarm cut through Penny's dream, yanking her out of sleep. Her heart pounded as the harsh sound filled the quiet room, disorienting her for a moment. She blinked groggily, trying to make sense of where she was and what had happened. Slowly, the pieces of the previous night began to fall into place.

She reached over to silence the alarm, letting the sudden quietness settle over her like a warm blanket. Memories trickled in, soft and comforting. She and Nathan had talked—*really* talked. The kind of raw, open conversation they hadn't had in what felt like forever. They'd stayed up late, both of them reluctant to let the moment end, the clock flashing 2:00 a.m. before they realized just how much time had passed.

A sleepy smile tugged at Penny's lips as she remembered making him a bed on the couch. It had felt right, the small kiss she'd given him goodnight before retreating to her own room, the kind of simple intimacy that had been missing for far too long.

Sitting up, she rubbed her eyes and glanced toward the window. The soft light of dawn was creeping through the blinds, casting muted shadows across her bedroom floor. Her body ached with exhaustion, but there was no time to linger. The day was already pulling her into its rhythm, the responsibilities of work looming on the horizon.

With a groan, she slipped out of bed, grabbing her phone as she made her way to the bathroom. The shower was warm, the steady stream of water soothing as it poured over her, waking her up bit by bit. Her mind wandered, replaying fragments of the night before. How Nathan had opened up, his voice low and raw, how they had navigated the vulnerability with care. It felt like a new beginning, but the guarded part of her wasn't ready to label it as such just yet.

She sighed, knowing her coworkers at the station would undoubtedly have a thousand questions. They already knew Nathan was coming over—*and* they were the type to jump to conclusions before she even got a word in. Penny chuckled softly to herself. She could already hear Walter's teasing and Chloe's concern, both wrapped up in the kind of banter that came from people who cared too much.

After a quick shower, she toweled off and slipped into a pair of jeans and a soft T-shirt. Her reflection in the mirror surprised her; she looked... calm. Calm despite the emotional whirlwind of the last few days. Her hair, still damp, twisted easily into a messy bun, and she tugged on a sweatshirt as she made her way out of the bedroom.

In the kitchen, she reached for a banana, her mind debating whether to leave Nathan a note or just quietly slip out. A part of her wanted to avoid any potentially awkward morning-after moments. But then again, there hadn't been any awkwardness last night. It had been better than she'd anticipated—comfortable, easy, even in the midst of all the heavy conversation.

The soft sound of movement from the living room made her pause. Nathan was awake. Her heart gave a small flutter of nerves, the kind that always came in those first quiet moments after a long night of emotional vulnerability. She had hoped to slip out unnoticed, but that plan was already slipping away.

She turned the corner and found him sitting on the couch, his hair tousled, his eyes still heavy with sleep. He looked up as she entered the room, a small smile playing at his lips.

"Morning," he said, his voice rough and low, as he rubbed his eyes.

Penny felt a warmth spread through her chest, unexpected but welcome. "Morning," she replied, leaning against the kitchen doorframe, the banana still in her hand. "Did the alarm wake you up?" she asked softly, giving him a small smile. "You can stay if you want to sleep a little more. Just lock up when you leave."

Nathan, sitting on the edge of the couch, looked up at her with a faint grin, running a hand through his messy hair. "Yeah, but it's fine. I should get going too," he replied, his voice still carrying that morning rasp. "Just give me a couple minutes, and I'll head out with you."

Penny watched him as he searched for his shoes, trying not to let her gaze linger too long. He seemed so comfortable in her home… almost as if he belonged there.

Suppressing the smile tugging at her lips, she pulled on

her sweatshirt, grabbed her bag, and made her way toward the door. She turned to glance back at him. "Are you sure you've got everything?" she asked, not even trying to hide the hint of warmth in her voice.

Nathan smiled, slipping his shoes on. "Yeah, I'm good," he said, pausing for a moment before adding, "Can I text you later? I know we covered a lot last night, but there's more I want to talk about. I just want to make sure we're on the same page. Is that okay?"

The sincerity in his voice sent a wave of something deep and steady through her. The conversation last night had been a start, but they were far from finished. She appreciated that he wasn't pretending everything had been fixed in a single night. They were both still standing on shaky ground, but the fact that he wanted to keep talking, keep working through it—that mattered.

Penny felt the weight of his words settle somewhere soft in her chest. "I'd like that," she said. "I'm not doing anything after work, so I'll be home around 2:30."

Nathan's face softened at her response, and he took a step closer, leaning in to press a soft kiss to her cheek. It was simple, barely more than a brush of his lips, but the tenderness behind it sent warmth spiraling through her. She caught herself holding her breath as she smiled faintly, turning to follow him out the door. The click of the lock behind them felt like a closing chapter and starting a new one—one she wasn't entirely sure how to feel about—but the sun was bright outside, and the world seemed just a little lighter.

As they stood by their cars, Penny felt an odd sense of peace settle over her. Nathan was back in her life, a part of her world again, but this time it felt different. There were still no guarantees, no promises etched in stone, but there was hope. And for the first time in weeks, Penny allowed herself to feel that hope, to hold it, even if just for a moment.

"Drive safe," she said as she unlocked her car, her fingers brushing over the cold metal of the handle.

Nathan smiled, leaning against his car door. "You too. I'll text you later."

Penny nodded, sliding into her seat and giving him a final glance before pulling out of the driveway. As she drove toward the station, the familiar routine of the morning commute creeping in, her thoughts began to wander. The cautious optimism she'd felt earlier wavered, and doubt started to creep in. Was she being naïve? Was this fragile reconnection built on something too unstable to last? Could they really move forward without falling back into the same patterns?

She shook her head, trying to silence the questions before they took root. They had made progress, and for now, that was enough. It had to be enough.

Penny pressed a little harder on the gas, the city rushing past her as the station came into view. One step at a time, she reminded herself. They'd figure out the rest when it came. But for now, the simple fact that they were both willing to try—*really* try—was enough to carry her through the day.

KEL SUMMERS

CHAPTER THIRTEEN

Later that afternoon, after dodging Chloe and Walter's relentless questions, Penny and was back at her house with Nathan. The tension from earlier still hung in the air, but now it felt different—less like anxiety and more like anticipation. They had already crossed the hardest part, the emotional storm of uncertainty, and now, as the late afternoon sun streamed through the windows, it felt like they were ready for the real conversation.

Nathan leaned back against the armrest of the couch, watching Penny as she moved about the room, gathering her thoughts. The notebook in her hand was a telltale sign that she had come prepared, and that thought made him smile. Penny was nothing if not thorough, and she did love her lists.

"It feels like we're finally on the same page," Penny said, turning to face him. She held the notebook up, a half-playful, half-serious expression crossing her face. "But, before we get too comfortable, I think we need to lay down some ground rules."

Nathan's lips twitched as he tried to suppress a grin. He wasn't surprised. Penny was meticulous. She was the kind of person who usually faced issues head-on. He liked that about her

—it was one of the things that had drawn him to her in the first place. And the notebook was classic Penny. He leaned forward, feigning seriousness as he nodded toward it. "Go on, hit me with it."

Penny stood up straighter, holding the notebook like it was a sacred text, her expression mock-serious. She cleared her throat dramatically. "First things first," she began, her eyes twinkling with amusement as she delivered her "rules" with theatrical flair, "we cannot make this harder than it needs to be. Relationships are going to hit rough patches—that's a given. But they become harder when we're not being true to ourselves or each other. That's why communication is key. If we don't keep the lines open, even when it's uncomfortable, we'll end up right back where we were."

Nathan's smile softened as he listened. Despite the playful delivery, he could hear the seriousness beneath her words. He leaned forward, resting his elbows on his knees. "I agree," he said quietly, the smile fading as her words sank in. "Communication's always been a sticking point for me. I thought it would be easy, but clearly, I've struggled with it. What else?"

Penny smirked, her eyes gleaming as she turned the notebook around to reveal a blank page. Nathan blinked at it for a second before bursting out laughing.

"That's it? I was expecting a whole top-ten situation," he teased, leaning back into the couch, his eyes crinkling with amusement.

Penny grinned, settling down beside him, her shoulder brushing against his as she leaned back, notebook forgotten on the coffee table. "There *are* other things," she admitted, her voice light. "Like respecting each other's space, never rubbing your cold feet on my legs—" Nathan snorted at that one "—and, of course, always putting the toilet seat down. But I figure if we can master communication, the rest of it should fall into place. I mean, we both have careers focused on communicating with people. We shouldn't have this much difficulty in our relationship."

Nathan's laughter filled the room. "Yeah, well," he said, smirking. "Talking to computers doesn't exactly prepare you for this."

But just as things began to settle into that warm familiarity, Penny's phone buzzed on the table, interrupting their moment. She glanced at it, her expression shifting slightly as she read the message. "Oh, it's Mark and Stacie," she said, eyes widening as she remembered. "I completely forgot we had plans to watch that new show tonight. They're on their way over."

Nathan tilted his head, watching her carefully. "You didn't tell them I'm back, did you?"

Penny bit her lip, a sheepish look crossing her face as she shook her head. "Nope, not yet. I was going to call them today, but... I just haven't."

Nathan let out a soft sigh, leaning back and crossing his arms. "I can see how that might be a little awkward," he said, his tone understanding. There was no anger or frustration in his voice, only calm reassurance. "How about this—I've got some work I can finish up at the newspaper office. There are a few things I still need to close out with the Seattle team anyway, so I can head to the hotel for the night. We can catch up again tomorrow."

Penny blinked, her mind struggling to catch up with Nathan's words. "Wait, you're closing things out in Seattle?" Her voice wavered slightly with confusion as she tried to piece it all together. She hadn't even considered the idea that he might be staying. In the back of her mind, she'd assumed that they would be navigating this new phase of their relationship long-distance, adding that extra layer of difficulty to an already fragile situation. "You're staying?"

Nathan's eyes softened as they met hers, and a small smile tugged at the corners of his lips. "Yeah," he said, his voice calm and steady. "You can add that to your list if you want. I'd like us to be in the same state. Maybe even the same town, if you want to get crazy." He paused, stepping closer, his tone growing more serious, almost vulnerable. "And maybe, if I can keep myself together this time... eventually, the same house. You know, if your grandmother gives me her blessing, of course." He glanced around the room and gave a small nod, as if the spirit of Penny's grandmother was watching over them.

Before Penny could respond, Nathan pulled her into a quick embrace and kissed her softly on the lips, his familiar warmth sending a flutter through her chest. And just like that, he was gone, the front door clicking softly behind him.

Penny stood there, frozen, her mind racing as she replayed his words. *The same house.* He wasn't just talking about sticking around. He was talking about building a future with her. The man who once couldn't leave fast enough, the man who ran from every possibility of a relationship, was now talking about living together. Her heart raced as the realization hit her fully. Nathan wasn't just here—he was serious.

Her thoughts swirled, emotions pulling her in every direction at once. Could she trust this? Could she trust him, after everything they'd been through? And yet, there was a part of her—quiet but steady—that dared to hope.

Before she could collect herself, the doorbell rang, yanking her back to reality. Penny shook her head, trying to clear the fog, and hurried to answer the door.

Penny swung open the door, her face lighting up as she greeted her two best friends. The ones who had been by her side through every twist and turn of her relationship with Nathan. "Hey, you two! Get in here."

Mark and Stacie stepped inside, immediately kicking off their shoes by the door. Mark stretched his arms, yawning dramatically. "Alright, what are we eating? I'm starving."

Stacie was already halfway to the fridge, pulling it open with familiar ease. "Let's see what you've got, Penny," she said, her voice muffled as she rummaged through the shelves. "There's got to be something here we can work with."

Mark leaned over Stacie's shoulder, peering into the fridge with a raised eyebrow. "Pickles, yogurt, and… is that a sad-looking bag of spinach? Not exactly a feast."

Stacie slammed the fridge door shut with a playful groan. "Guess it's takeout then. Chinese or pizza?"

Penny smiled absently, leaning against the counter. She

wasn't fully paying attention to their banter. Her mind was elsewhere, replaying the conversation she'd had with Nathan earlier. His words echoed in her head, a mix of excitement and uncertainty tugging at her heart.

"Penny?" Stacie's voice snapped her out of her reverie, pulling her back to the moment.

"Huh? Oh, sorry, yeah... takeout sounds great," Penny mumbled, brushing a loose strand of hair behind her ear. She forced a smile, but both Mark and Stacie exchanged curious glances, sensing that something was off.

"You okay?" Mark asked, tilting his head as he reached for his phone. "You seem a little... distracted."

Penny gave a quick nod, trying to shake off her lingering thoughts. "Yeah, I'm fine. Just... a lot on my mind," she said, her voice trailing off.

Thirty minutes later, they were sprawled across the couch, boxes of Chinese takeout scattered haphazardly on the coffee table. The three of them had settled into their usual routine —talking, eating, and watching the latest show they'd been meaning to check out. But Penny wasn't fully engaged. She kept waiting for the right moment to bring up Nathan, but every time she thought about saying something, the words got stuck. She didn't know how to tell them. Didn't know if she was ready to handle their reactions.

They finished the first episode, critiquing it as they went, debating whether to give it another chance or delete it from their watchlist. Penny laughed along with them, but her heart wasn't in it. She was stalling, and she knew it. The knots in her stomach tightened as she stared at the TV, contemplating whether or not to just blurt it out.

Mark caught her staring into space again. "Okay, seriously, what's up?" he asked, leaning forward, his eyes narrowing with concern. "You've been a little off all night. Spill."

Penny swallowed hard, the weight of the moment pressing down on her. She couldn't keep it in any longer. Taking a deep breath, she grabbed the remote and clicked the TV off, plunging the room into silence.

"Okay," she began, her voice quieter than usual. "There's something I need to tell you guys."

Stacie and Mark exchanged a glance, both of them sitting up a little straighter, sensing that whatever was coming next wasn't going to be small.

Penny bit her lip, hesitating for a brief second before finally letting out a shaky breath. "Nathan's back," she began, her voice steady but her heart racing. "And he wants to stay."

For a moment, there was silence. Stacie's eyes widened slightly, while Mark's expression remained unreadable.

Stacie was the first to speak. "Wait, like… *staying* staying? As in, not going back to Seattle?"

Penny nodded, her heart pounding in her chest. "Yeah. He told me today he's closing things out there. He wants to be here. With me. He's… he's even talking about us living together."

Stacie's jaw dropped, her eyes widening in shock. "Hold on—*living together*? Like, in this house?"

"Yeah, here." Penny let out a small laugh, still trying to wrap her own head around the idea. "He mentioned asking my grandma for permission, so... yeah, he's serious."

Mark leaned back against the couch, crossing his arms over his chest. "Wow. That's... big." He looked at her closely, his voice careful. "How do you feel about it?"

Penny let out a shaky laugh, her hands twisting together in her lap. "I don't know," she admitted. "I mean, I'm happy. I think. I just... I didn't expect things to move this quickly, you know? But I guess if I'm honest with myself, I've wanted this for a while. I just didn't think it would happen so soon."

Stacie leaned over, placing a hand on Penny's arm, her voice soft but firm. "Do you love him?"

Penny didn't hesitate. "Yes," she said, her voice steady. "I do. I just... I don't want to get hurt again."

Stacie fidgeted uneasily on the couch, glancing between Penny and Mark. She took a deep breath before finally speaking. "Okay, I've got to be honest here... I'm kind of rooting for him." She balled her fist and held it up in front of her face as if preparing for an onslaught of reactions from Mark. Her expression was a mix of sheepishness and defiance. "I mean, yeah, Nathan's definitely a bit damaged. He's made some questionable choices, no doubt. But... I think he was just trying to protect himself. I don't like that he hurt you, Penny, but I also think he loves you. Really loves you."

Mark shot her a mock glare, crossing his arms as he leaned back into the couch, eyebrows raised in playful indignation. "Gah. Since when did you start making sense? That's usually my job in this trio."

Penny let out a soft chuckle, grateful for the way they always managed to lighten the mood, even when her thoughts were weighed down by uncertainty. She shifted in her seat, her eyes softening as she looked between her two best friends. "Once we actually talked, I kind of felt the same way," she admitted, her fingers absentmindedly toying with the edge of her sleeve. "Yeah, he messed up. He really messed me up by not being honest about his feelings, but... I remember what I was like after Jeremy ended things. I was barely myself. It took me forever to trust again, and I almost didn't let Nathan in because of that. So, I get it. I can't hold his fears against him."

Stacie leaned forward, her curiosity getting the best of her. "So... you talked, he was here earlier... does that mean you guys are officially back on? Is he going to be back on the show with you? What's next?"

Penny twisted the end of her ponytail around her finger, her gaze dropping to the floor as she weighed her answer. The uncertainty still hung in the air, but it didn't feel as suffocating now. "It's... complicated," she said slowly, her voice steady but tinged with the reality of the situation. "He told me he's coming back to town, that he's done with Seattle. But as for the rest? We're taking it one day at a time. There's still a lot we need to figure out, and honestly, I hadn't even thought about him coming back to the show."

Mark leaned in, resting his elbows on his knees as he locked eyes with Penny. "The most important question, though—are *you* happy?" His tone was serious, but his expression softened with genuine concern. "Because if you're happy, that's what really matters. You can figure out the rest later. But if this guy isn't making you happy, I'll personally make him disappear." His voice was only half-joking.

They all laughed, causing the rest of the tension to ease from the room. Penny smiled, feeling the warmth of their support wash over her. "I don't need him to disappear," she said, rolling her eyes. "But thanks for the offer. Really."

he three of them sat back, falling into an easy rhythm. They peppered Penny with lighthearted questions, each one tinged with the care and concern only close friends could offer. Penny was surprised by how well they were taking the news, and as they bantered back and forth, she realized just how lucky she was to have them by her side. Their acceptance of Nathan's return didn't feel like judgment—it felt like support. And that made her feel even more confident in the decision she was making.

An hour later, after Mark and Stacie had left, Penny moved through the house, tidying up the remnants of their evening together. As she straightened the cushions on the couch, her mind replayed the conversation with her friends. Their easygoing acceptance had lifted a weight off her shoulders she hadn't realized she was carrying. A small smile tugged at her lips as she pulled out her phone and quickly typed a message to Nathan.

Penny: *Hey! Just finished up with Mark and Stacie.*

> *I told them everything, and... they handled it way better than I thought they would. Mark joked about making you disappear if I wasn't happy, but Stacie? She's kind of rooting for you.*

She hit send, and resumed tidying, the soft buzz of her phone coming almost immediately.

> **Nathan:** *Rooting for me? Wow! I didn't see that one coming. Glad it went well, though. I was worried they might still hate me.*

Penny laughed as she read his response, quickly typing back.

> **Penny:** *No hate, just a lot of protective vibes. They're in full "don't mess with our girl" mode, but honestly, I think they're happy for us. I feel lighter, actually.*

Nathan's reply buzzed in again.

> **Nathan:** *I'm really glad to hear that. I've been on edge thinking they'd be giving you a hard time. Can I see you tomorrow?*

Penny's heart did a little flip as she read his message. She paused before responding, thinking about how much better she felt after getting everything out in the open with her friends.

> **Penny:** *Yeah, I'd like that. I'm free after work. Come by my place—around 5:30?*

> **Nathan:** *Perfect. Can't wait to see you. Good night,*

Penny.

Penny smiled, warmth spreading through her chest as she replied.

Penny: *Sleep well, Nathan. Talk tomorrow.*

Later, as she changed into her pajamas and settled into bed, Penny felt a sense of peace she hadn't felt in a long time. Her mind drifted to the future—the future she was finally allowing herself to imagine with Nathan. The thought of them living together didn't seem as daunting as it had earlier in the evening, though the pace of it all still made her heart race a little. But it felt right, in the ways that mattered most.

As Penny snuggled deeper into the covers, her heart lighter than it had been in what felt like forever, she counted her blessings, letting each one soothe her worries. She smiled to herself as she drifted off, knowing that for now, things were exactly as they were supposed to be.

CHAPTER FOURTEEN

The morning light filtered through the blinds of the studio as Penny sat behind the microphone, sipping her coffee and scanning the notes for today's show. The studio had the familiar hum of quiet activity, the producers in their corner, the soft shuffle of papers, and the occasional beep of equipment.

She heard the door creak open and turned just as Jake hurried inside, his face slightly flushed, looking like he'd sprinted across the building. He dropped into the chair next to her with mere minutes to spare before they went live.

"Made it just in time," he said, grinning as he ran a hand through his tousled hair, trying to catch his breath.

Penny smiled, shaking her head. "Cutting it close, huh?"

"Always do," Jake replied with a wink. "So… we didn't get a chance to talk about it yesterday, but… what do you think? Do you see Nathan coming back to the show? Or has that ship sailed?"

Penny hesitated, chewing her lip. "Funny you should mention that. Mark and Stacie asked the same thing last night. Honestly, I don't know. He hasn't mentioned it. We were more focused on figuring out our personal lives, so our professional lives didn't even come up. I wonder how our fans would react if he came back. I think some of them took the news of our break-up worse than I did." Penny joked.

Jake nodded, watching her closely. "I get it. You guys have a lot to figure out." He glanced over at the script, then back at her. "But you know... the show's been a little different without him. The new format's good, but it hasn't taken off the way we thought it would. Don't get me wrong—I'm all for going lighter and more positive. But sometimes, the listeners want a bit of drama. You know, spice things up a little."

Penny chuckled, though the weight of the situation lingered in the back of her mind. "Yeah, I get it. And I won't lie, the whole Nathan-Penny drama definitely kept things interesting. It probably would have kept the ratings sky-high for weeks."

Jake smirked, pointing a finger at her as if she'd struck gold. "Exactly. You nailed it."

She shook her head, feeling the weight of the decision. "The thing is... I don't even know how to bring it up to him. There's so much we're still working through. Maybe Ruth or William could help nudge things in the right direction? How is he feeling, by the way?"

"He's doing a lot better," Jake said, a note of relief in his voice. "Back home from the hospital, finally. Resting, but he's not the kind of guy who stays still for long, you know? Probably driving Ruth crazy."

Penny smiled. "I'm glad to hear that."

Jake paused, then leaned forward again, his tone more serious. "Look, Penny. Before we even talk to Ruth or anyone else, I think you have to ask yourself if you even want him back on the show. I mean, you two have always had great chemistry, but this would put your relationship back on display, front and center."

Penny nodded slowly, her gaze dropping back to the script. He was right. They hadn't even scratched the surface of what it meant to be together again, let alone what it would mean to work side by side. "I think I need time to figure that out," she said quietly. "This isn't just about what's good for the show. It's about what's good for us. Can I think about it?"

Jake nodded slowly. "Of course, of course," he said as the show's theme music started to play, signaling the start of the broadcast. "We'll talk again in a couple of days." He gave her a reassuring smile as he backed out of the room.

Later, as Penny drove home, her thoughts returned to her conversation with Jake. They had agreed to wait before bringing up Nathan's return to Ruth, but there was still so much to consider. The thought of working with Nathan again, especially after everything they had been through, was both exciting and terrifying.

She glanced at her phone, smiling at his earlier message asking if he could cook dinner. Did he not know her at all? Someone offering to cook for her would always get a yes vote, especially if they were a good cook, which he was.

She stepped out of the car, her heels clicking lightly on the driveway as she spotted Nathan already unloading groceries from his trunk. His tall frame stood silhouetted by the setting sun, and when he turned to greet her, his face broke into a boyish grin.

"Need some help?" she called, swinging her bag over her shoulder.

"Always." He chuckled, holding out a bag for her. "I just grabbed a few things for tonight. Thought I'd cook your favorite."

Penny peered into the bag, her eyes lighting up. "Wine, pasta, and... fresh mushrooms? Marsala?" She gave him a playful, knowing look.

"I'm hoping it might win me some extra points tonight," he said, before giving her a quick kiss.

They carried the bags inside, and Penny felt a sense of peace wash over her as she kicked off her shoes and headed to change. After slipping into a pair of cut-offs and an old concert tee, she reappeared in the kitchen, where Nathan had already opened a bottle of wine and set two glasses on the counter.

"I could get used to this," she said, taking a sip of the wine. She leaned against the counter, watching as Nathan placed a pot on the stove, his attention focused on preparing the meal.

"How was your day?" Nathan asked over his shoulder. "Any feedback from the team on, well... us?"

Penny's heart skipped a beat. She hadn't expected him to bring it up so casually. She swirled her wine glass, the liquid catching the light as she gathered her thoughts. "Funny you ask," she began. "Jake did. He mentioned how the new format isn't... well, it's not exactly the hit we thought it would be. Then he asked if you'd ever consider coming back to the show."

Nathan's hand stilled over the pot for a moment before he turned to face her, his expression thoughtful. Penny studied him, wondering what he might say. Part of her regretted bringing it up so soon, but she knew they had to talk about it sooner or later. And they'd promised to talk about things, even if the conversations were uncomfortable.

"I've been thinking about that too," Nathan admitted, leaning back against the counter, crossing his arms. "I didn't want to bring it up until I knew where we stood, though."

Penny raised an eyebrow, surprised by his candor. "And... how do you feel about it?" She hesitated. "I mean, I love working with you, Nathan. We're good together—when we're not actively trying to mess things up," she added with a soft smile. "But I don't want to put any pressure on us. We're just figuring things out again, and throwing ourselves back into the spotlight... I don't know. It feels risky."

Nathan's gaze softened, and he took a step toward her. Gently, he reached out, brushing a strand of hair from her face, his fingers lingering for just a second longer. "Penny," he said, his voice low, "if we do this—if I come back—it's going to be on our terms. The show, the job, it's important, but it's not *us*. What we're building is. We'll keep talking, and we won't let it pull us apart. I promise you that."

A sense of relief washed over her, and Penny nodded,

exhaling the tension she hadn't realized she was holding. "I don't want to lose what we're rebuilding," she whispered.

"You won't," Nathan assured her, his voice steady. "We won't let that happen."

For a moment, they just stood there, the warmth of the kitchen surrounding them like a protective bubble. The smell of the food on the stove mingled with the quiet peace that had settled between them, and Penny felt a flicker of hope—a hope she hadn't let herself feel for weeks.

"I'm glad you're here," she said softly, stepping closer, resting her head against his chest.

Nathan wrapped his arms around her, pulling her into a gentle embrace, resting his chin lightly on top of her head. "There's nowhere else I'd rather be," he whispered. After a pause, he added, "I talked with my family today."

Penny pulled back slightly, looking up at him. "Oh? About what?"

Nathan exhaled, his eyes searching hers before he spoke. "My cousin, the one they brought in to replace me at the paper when I left for Seattle… he's stepping down. Said he's not that into the news business anymore. Which means… the position's open, if I want it."

Penny blinked, processing what he was saying. "And do you? Do you want it?"

Nathan hesitated, running a hand through his hair as if trying to sort through the jumble of thoughts in his head. "I think so," he said finally. "The paper needs stability, someone who's actually invested in it. And since I'm staying… putting down roots here, then it's time to settle on a clear career path. I can't keep bouncing back and forth between technology and communications. It has to be one or the other."

The weight of his words lingered in the quiet kitchen, like an unspoken promise hovering between them. Penny, sensing the gravity of what he was saying, set her wine glass on the counter. The clink of the glass against the marble sounded louder than usual in the otherwise still room. She moved a little closer to him

"And how do you feel about that? Really?" Her voice was gentle but held a quiet urgency, like she was searching his face for the truth beneath his words. "Where's your heart in all of this, Nathan?"

Nathan looked down for a moment, then back up at her with those familiar blue eyes, now clouded with thought. "I've been thinking about it a lot," he admitted, his tone raw. "I can't keep living in fear—fear of getting hurt again, fear of things falling apart before they even have a chance to begin." His voice dropped slightly, more introspective now. "I know how I feel about you, Penny. That's the one thing that's been clear through all of this, even when I refused to see it."

Her heart did a little flip at his confession, but she stayed silent, letting him process aloud. She could see the struggle he'd been carrying, the weight of trying to balance his ambitions, fears, and love for her all at once.

Nathan took a step closer to her, the space between them

shrinking. "It's time for me to take a leap of faith," he said quietly, but with conviction. "Because I know without a doubt, I can't lose you again."

Penny felt a lump form in her throat, a mixture of relief, hope, and a deep understanding of what this moment meant for both of them. She smiled softly, leaning back against the counter, tracing the rim of her glass absentmindedly, trying to ground herself in the simplicity of this moment.

"It sounds like you're planting some roots then," she said, keeping her voice light. There may have been a teasing edge to her words, but beneath it was the undeniable affection she held for him.

Nathan, standing just inches from her, reached out and brushed a stray lock of hair from her face. "Like a tree," he said, his lips tugging into a faint smile. "I've got this."

Then, leaning forward, he pressed a soft kiss to her forehead, the kind of kiss that wasn't about passion but about reassurance, a quiet promise that said more than any words could. She closed her eyes, letting the intimacy of the moment wash over her. It was a moment built on trust, on the promise of commitment, and the choice to leap together into the unknown.

The kitchen seemed to cocoon them in that moment, the hum of the refrigerator was the only sound breaking the stillness. When Nathan pulled back slightly, his hand lingering on her waist, Penny looked up at him, her eyes bright with the affection she no longer felt the need to hide.

"Good," she whispered, her voice carrying all the weight of

her own emotions. "Because I want to grow roots with you."

Nathan's smile deepened, his eyes crinkling at the edges as he pulled her into his arms, holding her close. There was no rush in his embrace, just the quiet assurance of two people choosing each other. The world outside felt far away, the challenges they would inevitably face seemed smaller now, less daunting, because in this moment, they had each other.

"I'm not going anywhere," Nathan murmured into her hair, his voice thick with emotion. "Not this time."

Penny rested her head against his chest, listening to the steady beat of his heart, and for the first time in a long time, she believed him. This was it. They were in it together… ready to take on whatever challenges, joys, and surprises life would throw their way.

KEL SUMMERS

CHAPTER FIFTEEN

Penny checked her phone, sighing as she pushed the covers back and swung her legs over the edge of the bed. Sleep had eluded her all night, her mind too busy cycling through thoughts and emotions. The nervous energy kept her tossing and turning, anticipation gnawing at her insides. She had never lived with anyone before, and today, that was about to change. Nathan was moving in. The reality weighed on her in a way she hadn't anticipated, but it also filled her with excitement.

They had talked about it endlessly over the past few weeks, hashing out every detail. Nathan couldn't keep living in a hotel, and he was already spending most nights in her guest room anyway. It was the next logical step—merging their lives. And when *Doubting Penny* would make an appearance, her family and friends gently reminded her that taking chances was a part of life and sometimes those chances were worth the risk.

With a yawn, she tied her hair into a messy bun and made her way into the kitchen. The house felt still, as if it was holding its breath for what was to come. Grabbing a muffin, Penny stood by the window, taking a bite and thinking about the day ahead. Chloe and Mark were on their way to help, leaving their cars at her place while Nathan picked up the U-Haul and officially checked out of the hotel. His things were packed in a nearby storage unit, and with the four of them working together, it shouldn't take long to move everything.

Stacie, originally eager to help, had to bow out at the last minute. Her boyfriend had surprised her with a weekend getaway, and Penny smiled at the thought of her friend lounging on a beach somewhere, even though Stacie had insisted on feeling guilty. Penny had brushed off the guilt easily, knowing that Dan was planning to propose. "Go have fun," she'd told her. "You've got a big weekend ahead."

Just as Penny finished her muffin, a knock at the door pulled her from her thoughts. Chloe and Mark arrived, their banter filling the quiet space before they even stepped inside. They had finally met a couple weeks ago at a promotional event for *A Penny for Your Thoughts* and had been almost inseparable ever since.

"You sure you want to live with that guy?" Chloe teased, nudging Penny with a grin, her eyes zeroing in on the half-eaten muffin in Penny's hand. "You could always keep your quiet little sanctuary here."

Penny smirked, brushing a crumb from her lip. "That guy cooks and cleans. I think I'll keep him."

Mark, rolling his eyes at the two of them, clapped his hands together dramatically. "Come on, you two. Let's get this show on the road before you start planning matching aprons."

Minutes later, they rounded the corner to see the U-Haul parked in front of the house. Nathan stood leaning casually against the truck, arms crossed, his face lighting up the moment he saw Penny. She jogged over, a quick kiss greeting him as she ignored the exaggerated eye rolls from Chloe and Mark.

"Alright," Penny said, her voice filled with determination. "Let's do this."

Nathan grinned, rubbing his hands together in mock excitement. "Ready for some heavy lifting?"

They immediately got to work. The four of them made quick progress, seamlessly hauling boxes from the storage unit to the truck then from the truck into the house, the day filled with laughter and light-hearted teasing.

"Here, let me help with that," Chloe called out, noticing Penny struggling with a particularly large box. "It's nearly as big as you."

Penny, grateful, let Chloe take one end. Together, they carried the box into the house, adding it to the growing stack in the spare room. The weather, which had been threatening rain all week, had mercifully held off, leaving them with clear skies and a cool breeze.

Nathan leaned against the U-Haul, wiping sweat from his brow. "Are we done yet? I swear I didn't have this much stuff when I moved out west."

Mark, lugging two boxes at once, smirked. "At least you don't have a ton of furniture. A couple of boxes? I can handle that."

Chloe, noticing Mark's slight flex as he carried the boxes, raised an eyebrow. "Show-off," she muttered playfully, nudging Penny. Penny chuckled, watching as Mark flashed Chloe a grin, clearly trying to impress her.

As they finished unloading, Penny took a step back, her gaze wandering over the house. The day's reality settled into her bones —the weight of it, the joy of it. Six months ago, Nathan had re-entered her life, and now they were finally merging their worlds under one roof. She had insisted on keeping her small house, and to her relief, Nathan hadn't pushed back. Together, they'd worked to make it feel like theirs, even renovating the attic to create a cozy shared office space. Everything was starting to fall into place.

Nathan had officially wrapped up his work in Seattle, convincing William to let him launch the digital platform for the family's newspaper. The new platform had gone live this week, and it was already earning rave reviews. Penny had been nervous meeting his family at the launch party, unsure how they'd feel about her after the infamous "airport ambush" had become family lore. But to her surprise, they had welcomed her with open arms, his mother even pulling her aside to thank her for bringing Nathan back into the fold.

As they packed the last box into the house, Penny caught Nathan's eye. He smiled, that warm, familiar smile that had once seemed so distant, so impossible to pin down. Now it was here, steady and real.

"How are you feeling about all this?" he asked, stepping toward her. "And please choose your words carefully, because it's too late to change your mind."

Penny laughed softly, leaning into him. "I'm feeling good. I told you before, you're stuck with me. And now? This makes it harder for you to escape."

He pulled her into a hug, resting his chin on her head. "There's nowhere else I'd rather be."

Mark's voice cut through the room, his teasing tone lighthearted but enough to break the comfortable bubble Penny and Nathan were wrapped in. "Can you two stop the lovey-dovey stuff and make sure we have everything unloaded? We didn't come here to star in a rom-com."

Penny laughed, giving Mark a mock glare as she shoved him lightly on the shoulder. "Yes, sir. Sorry to flaunt our happiness all over *our* house."

The words slipped out naturally, and as soon as they did, Penny felt her chest flutter. *Our house.* It was the first time she'd said it like that, and the realization hit her with a mix of excitement and nervousness. She glanced at Nathan, curious to see if he had caught the emphasis.

Nathan's eyes locked with hers from across the room, and his expression softened into that familiar, warm smile that sent a rush of reassurance through her. He had definitely caught it. His smile said everything—this felt right. The house was becoming theirs, not just a place for Penny to call home but for Nathan too. She thought of her grandmother then, of the quiet comfort she still felt in this house, her presence lingering in the walls, in the air. Penny had always said her grandmother was still watching over her, and Nathan had never questioned it. In fact, they often joked about it.

"Your grandma's cool with me being here, right?" Nathan

had teased once, half-joking but also respectful of how connected Penny was to her family's past.

"Cool? She'd probably like you more than me," Penny had shot back with a grin, brushing her hand over the kitchen counter where her grandmother used to stand while baking. "She was always partial to the men who could cook."

And now, here they were, standing in what was no longer just *Penny's* space. It was *theirs*.

Nathan twisted the cap off a bottle of water and handed it to her, his touch gentle, his eyes lingering on her just a moment longer than necessary before he turned and offered water to Mark and Chloe. "Thanks again for all the help today," he said, his voice sincere. "I know helping friends move isn't anyone's idea of a fun way to spend a Saturday. We're ordering pizza if you two want to stick around."

Chloe took the water with a smile, shrugging off his thanks. "I'll have to take a rain check. I'm watching my niece tonight. My sister and brother-in-law have their date night, and it gives me an excuse to spent time with her and spoil her rotten."

Mark raised an eyebrow, his expression softening as he looked at Chloe. "Mind if I tag along? I love kids."

Chloe blinked, clearly caught off guard, but quickly recovered, flashing him a bright smile. "Sure! You'd love Tilly. She's eight—super smart and curious about everything. I'm trying to soak up as much time with her as possible before she turns into a sassy teenager. But I'm determined to stay the cool aunt, even through the teenage years."

Mark grabbed his keys from the counter, nodding. "I'm parked behind you, so I'll walk out with you. Nathan, I'll have to pass on the pizza, too. Maybe we can grab that beer sometime soon? When the girls do their next girls' night?"

Nathan nodded with an easy grin. "Definitely. Let's make it happen."

As Chloe and Mark made their way out the door, Penny stood by, watching them disappear down the driveway. She couldn't help but notice the way Mark had looked at Chloe—there was something there, subtle but unmistakable. The connection between them was undeniable, and Penny filed that observation away for later. It wasn't the first time she'd noticed, but they were both experts at keeping their cards close to their chests. She smiled to herself, imagining the conversation she'd have with Chloe when the time was right.

The door clicked softly behind them, leaving the house quiet once more. Penny turned to find Nathan leaning against the kitchen counter, his eyes following her as she approached. There was a softness between them now, an intimacy that came not from grand gestures but from the quiet understanding that they were beginning something real.

"You think they'll ever admit they like each other?" Penny mused, leaning against the counter beside him, her tone light but her mind still turning over the look she had just witnessed between her two friends.

Nathan chuckled, shaking his head. "Nah, not until they're both eighty and need someone to help with the crossword puzzles."

Penny laughed, the sound filling the room and easing any last bit of tension that had lingered. "Maybe. But I'll make sure it doesn't take them that long."

Nathan looked at her, his smile softening. "You know, watching you with them today… seeing you with your friends, the way you bring people together—it's one of the reasons I love you."

His words caught her off guard, the simple sincerity of them making her heart skip a beat. She met his gaze, feeling the depth of his words sink in. "You don't have to say things like that just because we're about to eat pizza in our new house," she teased, trying to keep things light, but her voice was a little shakier than she intended.

Nathan moved closer, his hand brushing lightly over her cheek. "I'm saying it because it's true. This is our home now, Penny. And I can't wait to keep building it with you."

She leaned into his touch, the warmth of his hand grounding her, making her feel both excited and safe in a way she hadn't realized she needed. "Our house," she echoed softly, letting the words roll off her tongue, letting them settle in her heart.

Nathan smiled, and for a moment, they stood there, the quiet weight of the moment wrapping around them like a blanket. Penny could feel it—this was real. The house, the future they were building together, all of it was real, and it was happening right now.

"Alright," she finally said, stepping back with a grin. "Let's see if your famous pizza-ordering skills are as good as your pasta-making skills."

Nathan laughed, grabbing his phone from the counter. "Prepare to be amazed."

KEL SUMMERS

CHAPTER SIXTEEN

Thirty minutes later, they were nestled on the couch, slices of pizza in hand and beers resting on the coffee table. The soft glow of the lamp filled the living room, casting warm shadows across the walls. A movie flickered on the TV, but neither of them was paying attention. The quiet intimacy between them was enough to fill the room.

Penny's eyes wandered over the space, finally landing on a small, brightly colored gift bag sitting on the table. She tilted her head in curiosity, her brow furrowing as she turned to Nathan. "What's this?" she asked, nodding toward the bag. "Shouldn't I be the one giving *you* a gift? A housewarming present or something?"

Nathan glanced at the bag and then flashed her a playful grin. "Oh, maybe. Didn't really think about that. I can take this one back if you want," he teased, his eyes gleaming with mischief.

Penny reached out and snatched the bag by its handle before he could make good on his mock offer. "Yeah, not happening," she said, her voice laced with anticipation.

Nathan leaned back against the couch, folding his arms as he watched her with a smile. He knew how much she loved surprises, and this moment was no exception. Penny carefully pulled out the tissue paper, tossing it aside with little fanfare, eager to see what was inside. Her fingers brushed against something familiar, and she couldn't help but let out a small laugh when she pulled it out.

A notebook.

Of course. He knew her so well. Penny had an obsession with notebooks, collecting them the way some people collected shoes. But this one felt different in her hands—weightier, as if it held more than just blank pages waiting to be filled.

She flipped open the cover, expecting to find the usual crisp, empty pages. Instead, her eyes landed on writing—a script that was not her own. Her brow furrowed again, and she glanced up at Nathan. He was watching her closely, his smile softer now, almost nervous. He shrugged, but there was a twinkle in his eyes that told her this wasn't just an ordinary gift.

Penny's gaze dropped back to the notebook, and her breath caught when she read the title scrawled across the first page: *Top Ten Reasons to Say Yes*.

Her heart fluttered in her chest as she realized what she was holding. It was his handwriting, his thoughts. The words were simple, unpolished, but deeply personal. She felt her pulse quicken as she began reading the list.

#1: You make me laugh even when I don't feel like smiling.

A smile tugged at the corner of her mouth.

#2: Every day I spend with you feels like an adventure, even the ordinary ones.

She paused, her heart swelling as she read the words. It wasn't just a list of reasons—it was a love letter, wrapped up in the familiarity of their shared moments, their jokes, their quiet talks late at night. Each reason brought back memories, and as she moved down the list, the emotions became almost overwhelming.

#3: You see the best in me, even when I can't.

#4: You give me a sense of home, wherever we are.

She felt her throat tighten as she continued to read. Each word felt more real, more vulnerable than the last. By the time she reached the final reason, Penny's breath hitched.

#10: Because I can't imagine my future without you.

Her hand trembled slightly as she closed the notebook, the weight of his words settling in her chest. She looked up at Nathan, her eyes wide with surprise, her mouth slightly open as she tried to process what she had just read. Before she could find the words, Nathan had already moved.

With a quiet rustle of fabric, Nathan dropped to one knee in front of her.

Penny gasped, her hand flying to her mouth in disbelief. Her heart raced, a flurry of hope, love, and shock filling her all at once. This was happening. Right here, right now.

Nathan's gaze held hers, steady and filled with an emotion so deep that it made her heart swell. "Penny," he began, his voice soft but filled with intention. "I've been thinking about this for a long time. I know I've been an idiot in the past, and I know I don't deserve the patience you've given me. But if there's one thing I've learned through everything we've been through... it's that I don't want to live another day without you by my side."

Penny's heart pounded in her ears. She felt like she was floating, yet completely grounded in this moment with him.

He reached into his pocket and pulled out a small, velvet box. Her eyes widened as he opened it, revealing a delicate ring. The light from the lamp caught on the diamond, casting tiny glimmers across the room, but Penny barely noticed. Her gaze was locked on him—on the man who had, through every twist and turn, become her person.

"I love you, Penny," Nathan continued, his voice catching slightly. "You've always been my person. And I want to spend the rest of my life proving that to you. Will you marry me?"

For a moment, everything seemed to still. The world outside, the movie playing in the background, even the ticking of the clock—it all faded away. All Penny could see was Nathan, all she could hear was the sound of her heartbeat and his words, hanging in the air like a promise.

Tears pricked at the corners of her eyes, and she felt a rush of emotion she hadn't expected. This man—this infuriating, lovable, complicated man—was asking her to share forever with him. And despite everything, despite the ups and downs, she knew her answer.

A smile broke across her face as she lowered her hand from her mouth, her eyes shining with unshed tears. "Yes," she whispered, her voice thick with emotion. "Yes, Nathan, I will marry you."

Nathan's face lit up, and before she could say another word, he wrapped her in his arms, pulling her into a deep, joyful kiss. Penny laughed against his lips, her heart soaring as she clung to him, feeling the warmth of his embrace, the certainty in his touch. When they finally pulled apart, her forehead rested against his, and they stayed like that for a moment, breathing in the reality of what had just happened.

"This feels right," Penny whispered, her voice barely audible but filled with all the love she had in her heart.

Nathan smiled, his thumb brushing her cheek. "It's more than right. It's everything."

And as they sat there, in the warm glow of their home, with the promise of forever stretching out before them, Penny knew that this was just the beginning of a beautiful new chapter.

KEL SUMMERS

CHAPTER SEVENTEEN

Two months later, under the shade of the apple trees that had stood proudly in her backyard for decades, Penny married the love of her life. The warm breeze rustled the leaves above, casting dappled sunlight over the small gathering of friends and family. The moment Nathan had asked her to marry him, there hadn't been a shred of doubt in her heart. After all the uncertainty and ups and downs they had faced at the beginning of their relationship, once they made the decision to commit, they never looked back.

Her bridesmaids—Stacie, Chloe, and Bonnie—were perfect, their brightly colored dresses contrasting against the soft, pastel palette of the day. They had taken turns over the last eight whirlwind weeks of planning, calming Penny's nerves when it all became too much. She smiled, knowing that as soon as she left for her honeymoon, they would probably take long naps to recover from the chaos.

When her father took her arm to walk her down the aisle, Penny felt a wave of emotion that threatened to overwhelm her. His eyes had misted over as they shared a quiet moment before the ceremony, his protective hand resting over hers, giving it a gentle squeeze. Once her parents had met Nathan, they'd instantly fallen for him, just as she had. Her dad had found a new golfing buddy in Nathan and Penny often joked that her father spent more time with Nathan than she did, especially on the golf course, where they seemed to lose hours together. But she didn't mind. Nathan had filled a space her father never knew he was missing—the son he never had—and as long as they kept knocking out the projects together on her ever-growing honey-do list, she wasn't going to complain.

Once they returned from their honeymoon—a quiet getaway to a cozy beach town—it was back to reality. Their daily lives resumed, but with a newfound depth. Nathan spent more time with her at the radio station, easing into a regular schedule alongside his work at the newspaper. His partnership with a cousin at the paper allowed him the freedom to finally pursue the digital platform he had long envisioned. It was a perfect balance of old and new, and Penny could tell the weight of his family's expectations was heavy but not overwhelming. He was handling it, just as she knew he would.

Their day-to-day life was everything Penny had hoped for. Sure, there were bumps, as there always are in any relationship, but Nathan kept true to his word. They always communicated, always worked through things. He never let anything fester, and if he ever felt overwhelmed, they took a step back and reset. It was one of the reasons Penny found herself falling deeper in love with him every day. She was grateful every day that she had given him another chance.

But life had its way of throwing surprises, and one afternoon, as she sat on her screened-in porch with her journal open in her lap, Penny couldn't shake the strange feeling in her stomach. It had been off for days now—long enough to make her wonder if something was wrong. She absentmindedly doodled in the margins of her notebook, her thoughts drifting from Nathan and her dad working on a project at her parents' house to her recent bout of strep throat, the exhaustion of which had lingered far longer than she'd expected.

The doorbell rang, pulling her from her thoughts. She wasn't expecting anyone, but that didn't mean much—Stacie and Chloe often popped by unannounced. With a sigh, she stood, pushing herself up from the couch and padding across the room to the door. But when she opened it, it wasn't Stacie or Chloe standing on her doorstep.

A delivery person stood there, holding a bouquet of vibrant Gerber daisies—her favorite.

"For me?" Penny asked, her voice tinged with surprise.

The delivery person nodded with a smile. "Yup. Enjoy!"

Penny grinned as she took the bouquet, her heart instantly swelling. *Nathan*, she thought. Of course, he had sent them. There was no occasion, no special reason, just him reminding her how much he loved her. It was moments like this that made her realize, again and again, why she had fallen for him so deeply.

She set the bouquet on the kitchen counter, still smiling as she admired the flowers. But before she could fully enjoy the moment, a wave of nausea hit her, sudden and sharp. She grimaced, her appetite disappearing entirely. She had been feeling off for a while now, and the discomfort was becoming too frequent to ignore. Reaching for the medicine cabinet, she paused, her fingers brushing against her birth control pack. A strange thought tugged at her, one she couldn't shake.

Had she missed a pill? No. She and Nathan had been careful. They weren't rushing into anything, especially not children. But something gnawed at her, a memory from a radio show they'd done months ago about surprise pregnancies. One of their guests had mentioned antibiotics interfering with birth control, and suddenly, it clicked. The strep throat, the antibiotics...

Penny's breath hitched. Could she be...?

Her mind raced. Pacing the kitchen, she grabbed her phone and quickly texted Stacie. *Can you run by the store and come over? Don't say anything to anyone else. I think I might be pregnant.*

Stacie's response was immediate, overflowing with emojis and excitement. *Coming now!!!!!*

Penny rolled her eyes, half amused, half panicked. It was easy for Stacie to be excited—she wasn't the one potentially carrying a surprise baby. Penny continued pacing, her thoughts whirling as she muttered under her breath, wondering if her grandmother was watching over her at that moment.

Fifteen minutes later, the doorbell rang again. This time, it was Stacie, standing on the doorstep with an armful of pregnancy tests. Penny blinked in disbelief.

"All of these?" she asked, raising an eyebrow.

"Better to be sure," Stacie grinned, her excitement practically bursting out of her. She shoved the tests into Penny's hands with a giggle. "Go on. Let's get this over with."

Penny hesitated, her nerves fraying at the edges. But Stacie, ever the determined friend, grabbed the instructions from Penny's hands. "Stop stalling. Just go take the test."

With a deep breath and her heart pounding, Penny made her way to the bathroom. Three minutes later, she stared at the test in her hand. The result was clear.

Positive.

She stepped out of the bathroom, her eyes wide, her mouth dry. Stacie squealed, bouncing up and down in excitement, but Penny could barely process what was happening.

"How am I going to tell Nathan?" she muttered, her voice shaky with uncertainty. Panic started to bubble up inside her. They were just getting settled. What if this threw everything off? What if it was too much?

Stacie placed a steadying hand on her shoulder, her voice soft but confident. "He's going to be excited, Penny. Trust me. You're both going to be amazing parents."

Penny nodded, trying to absorb her friend's reassurance, but the anxiety still lingered. She wanted to believe Stacie, wanted to share that same excitement. But as she stared at the positive test in her hand, all she could think about was how much their lives were about to change—and whether or not Nathan was ready for that change.

KEL SUMMERS

CHAPTER EIGHTEEN

Penny stood at the door for a moment longer, watching as Stacie's car disappeared down the street. The quiet settled back into the house, but her heart was still racing. When her phone buzzed, she glanced down and saw Nathan's text flash across the screen in bold, bright letters: *On my way home.*

Her stomach twisted. How was she going to tell him? She had spent the past hour pacing, running through countless scenarios with Stacie, trying to figure out the perfect way to say the words that would change their lives forever. No matter how many times she rehearsed it, the enormity of it still felt impossible to convey.

Taking a deep breath, Penny sat down on the couch, sinking into the worn cushions. The familiar fabric beneath her fingers usually brought comfort, but today it did little to calm the nervous energy vibrating inside her. She tried to focus on her surroundings, the soft glow of the afternoon light filtering through the curtains, the faint sound of birds chirping outside—but everything seemed distant, overshadowed by the weight of the moment.

As her gaze wandered aimlessly around the room, something caught her eye. There, just peeking out from beneath one of the shelves, was a book. Penny furrowed her brow That hadn't been there earlier, had it? She stood up, curiosity driving her, and walked over, crouching down to pull the book free.

Her breath hitched when she saw the cover. It was one of her grandmother's old books, the one she used to read to Penny when she was little. The edges were frayed from years of handling, but the faded cover still carried the warmth of the memories, as if it had been waiting for her to find it. Penny hadn't seen this book in years.

Sitting back down, she cradled the book in her lap, feeling an ache in her chest. Her grandmother's voice echoed in her mind, soft and melodic, the way she used to sing Penny to sleep after reading from this very book. Tears welled in her eyes, not from sadness but from the sense that, somehow, her grandmother was still here, watching over her, just as she always had.

Penny wiped her eyes quickly, placing the book gently on the coffee table. It felt like a sign—like her grandmother was reminding her that everything was going to be okay. She needed that assurance now more than ever.

A rumble outside broke through her thoughts. Nathan's car.

Her heart pounded faster as she heard his footsteps approach the door. The doorknob turned, and Nathan stepped inside, his face lighting up as he saw her. But the second he caught sight of her pale, tense expression, his smile faltered.

"Penny, are you okay?" Concern etched itself into his

features as he closed the door behind him and dropped his bag by the entrance. He crossed the room in a few quick strides, kneeling beside her on the couch. "You look a little pale. You're not getting sick again, are you? Did you eat anything today? Why don't I make you some soup?"

His hand rested lightly on her knee, the warmth of his touch grounding her, but also amplifying the nervous energy she'd been trying to hold back.

Penny let out a shaky breath, her fingers gripping the edge of the couch. "I'm fine... I mean, I'm not sick, exactly," she said, her voice wavering. "But there's something we need to talk about."

Nathan's brow furrowed, the lightness in his expression fading as he studied her more closely. "You're being weird," he said, half-joking, but there was an edge of unease in his tone now. "What's going on? You're making me nervous."

Penny swallowed hard, trying to steady herself. She'd been rehearsing this moment in her head for hours, but now that it was here, the words felt heavy, tangled in her throat. "Okay... So, I've been feeling a little off the past few mornings," she began, forcing herself to meet his gaze. "At first, I thought it was just stress or maybe something I ate. But then I started thinking... it might be something else."

Nathan's eyes narrowed, confusion clouding his features. "Something else?"

She nodded, her heartbeat thudding in her ears. "So... I asked Stacie to go to the store earlier and pick up something for me." Penny reached over to the coffee table and grabbed the box, holding it out to Nathan.

He took it, his eyes widening as he processed what he was holding. A pregnancy test. His mouth opened slightly, his gaze flickering back and forth between the box and her face. "A pregnancy test?" His voice cracked with disbelief. "Wait... are you saying—are we...?"

Penny nodded, her heart in her throat. "We are... pregnant."

For a moment, Nathan just stared at the box in his hands, his expression unreadable as he tried to make sense of it. Penny's nerves tightened as the silence stretched between them, but then —suddenly—his face broke into a wide grin, his eyes sparkling with excitement. "Are you serious?" he exclaimed, dropping the box and pulling her into his arms. "Penny, this is amazing! Are you really pregnant? This isn't some kind of joke, right? Please don't tell me this is a joke."

Penny laughed, the sound bubbling up from a place of pure relief. "No joke," she assured him, wrapping her arms around his neck. "I'm pregnant."

Nathan pulled back just enough to look into her eyes, his hands cupping her face gently. His voice softened, becoming almost reverent. "I've always wanted to be a dad," he whispered. "I didn't want to push you or anything, but... this is more than I ever could have hoped for."

Her chest swelled with emotion, the last of her fears melting away in the warmth of his words. "You're handling this a lot better than I expected," she admitted with a soft smile. "I mean, I was freaking out all day. But now that it's real... I think I'm excited too."

Nathan's thumb brushed gently across her cheek, his smile growing. "Holy cow, we're going to be parents."

EPILOGUE

"Happy birthday, dear Emily, happy birthday to you!" The room echoed with cheerful voices, a chorus of family and friends gathered around the tiny birthday girl. Emily, seated in her highchair like a princess on her throne, wasted no time smashing her chubby hands into the pink cake in front of her. The sight of Emily erupting into tiny giggles as she smeared icing across her rosy cheeks sent the entire room into laughter.

Penny stood nearby, her hands clasped in front of her, smiling as she took it all in. The laughter, the mess, the joy—it was almost overwhelming. She couldn't quite believe that her little girl was already one. How had a whole year flown by so quickly? Emily had been a tiny, delicate bundle in her arms just yesterday, or so it seemed. Now, she was a lively, curious toddler, gleefully making a mess of her first birthday cake.

"Thank goodness Mom insisted on putting that tablecloth under the highchair," Penny muttered to herself, laughing quietly as she wiped a bit of stray icing from her own cheek. Her mother's practical advice was still as golden as ever. The warmth of the afternoon sun filtered through the backyard, and Penny marveled at just how much life had changed.

As she looked around the room, her thoughts traveled back to five years ago when Nathan had returned from Seattle, uncertain and apologetic, but ready to fight for them. If someone had told her then that they would end up here, with a thriving radio show, two beautiful children, and a book in the works, she would've laughed them out of the room. But here they were, stronger than ever. Each memory they had created in their cozy home flashed through her mind.

The backyard, now filled with laughter, was the same place she had stood under the apple trees, her heart full, marrying the man of her dreams. Those very trees, planted with her grandmother so many years ago, stood tall and strong, much like the life she and Nathan had built together. They had found out about both pregnancies in the living room, the same room where Charlie had taken his first steps, and she had rocked Emily during many sleepless nights. Life had a way of surprising her, and Penny couldn't help but feel like she was living a dream—one she didn't want to wake from.

Her gaze landed on Nathan, standing a few feet away, helping to capture the moment on camera. He was beaming, as proud as ever. Her Superman, as she liked to call him. He caught her eye, and for a split second, time seemed to freeze. In that simple exchange, a whole conversation passed between them—gratitude, love, and a silent promise of everything yet to come. Penny smiled, her heart swelling with happiness.

The sound of Chloe's voice snapped Penny out of her thoughts. "Penny, can Charlie and Emily have some ice cream?" Chloe called from the kitchen, holding an ice cream scoop, her eyes twinkling as she glanced toward the kids.

"Just a small scoop," Penny replied, amused. "The cold still freaks Emily out a little, and I'm pretty sure Charlie's already had enough sugar for one day." She watched Chloe and Mark navigate around the kids, Mark bending down to help Charlie as he lingered near their feet, ever the protective big brother.

Penny watched the two of them, her heart warm. She had always suspected that Chloe and Mark had a spark between them, and now, watching them together, it was hard to imagine a time when they hadn't been a couple. The way they exchanged knowing glances, their playful banter—it was clear they were meant for each other. Penny smiled, her thoughts wandering to the quiet wedding they'd had just last month on Mark's family farm. It had been simple, beautiful, and so perfectly them.

Suddenly, a familiar squeal rang out from the front door, breaking through the chatter. "Oh. My. Goodness. Look how big she is!"

Penny's eyes lit up as she spotted Stacie walking through the door, her familiar energy filling the room. She rushed over, pulling her friend into a warm hug. "I'm so happy to see you!" Penny exclaimed, squeezing her tightly before pulling back. "Did Dan come too?"

Stacie grinned, brushing her hair out of her face. "Yes, he's just parking the car. You have quite the turnout here! I'm sorry I haven't made it back down until now."

Penny waved off her apology, leading her further into the house. "Don't worry about that. You're here now, and that's all that matters. How's the practice going? The new house? Do you get to stay for a little while? FaceTime just doesn't cut it anymore—we need real catch-up time!"

Stacie laughed, nodding as she glanced around at the buzzing crowd. "We actually got a hotel for the night. I begged and pleaded, even threw a little tantrum. Stomped my foot once or twice to get Dan on board." Her voice was teasing, but Penny could see the excitement in her eyes.

"You're staying?" Penny practically squealed. "That's wonderful news! We'll have time to really catch up."

Before Stacie could reply, Nathan appeared beside them, wrapping his arm casually around Penny's waist while using his other to give Stacie a quick hug. "Stacie! Thanks for coming. Is Dan here?" he asked as he looked over her shoulder.

Stacie shot him a playful look, her lips curling into a smirk. "Now see, when Penny asks that, she's just being polite. But when you ask, I see new golf clubs or a stereo system in my husband's future."

Laughter erupted between them as Penny shook her head. It was true. Nathan and Dan had clicked from the moment they met. Penny and Stacie often joked that the two of them were worse than they ever were. When Nathan and Dan were together, it was impossible to get a word in, and the way they obsessively compared gadgets and new toys made them seem like kids on Christmas morning. Add Mark into the mix, and the three of them became a force to be reckoned with.

"I swear, they're ten times worse than us," Penny teased,

nudging Stacie with her elbow.

Stacie rolled her eyes with a knowing grin. "Trust me, they don't agree." Her gaze flicked toward the front door as Dan finally made his way inside, giving Nathan a friendly handshake before the two disappeared into the crowd in search of Mark.

"Come on," Penny said, looping her arm through Stacie's and pulling her deeper into the party. As they wandered through the kitchen, Penny spotted Emily nestled in her mom's arm. Emily's eyelids drooped, her tiny head resting on her grandma's shoulder, cheeks still dotted with remnants of birthday cake.

Penny's heart swelled at the sight. There was something so tender about seeing her daughter snuggled up with her parents. Her mom caught her eye and flashed her a knowing smile, one that spoke of all the years of motherhood Penny had yet to experience.

"I think I'm going to have my hands full with this one," Penny quietly said, as she gently stroked her daughter's back.

Her mom nodded with a soft laugh. "She's your little firecracker, but she's perfect just the way she is."

Penny smiled warmly, watching as her mother rocked Emily back and forth in a slow rhythm. Charlie, her oldest, was curled up in his grandpa's lap, content as ever. She couldn't help but marvel at how different her two children were. Charlie had always been calm, easy-going, the type of kid who made parenting feel like a breeze. But Emily? She had come into the world with a burst of energy, challenging Penny in ways she hadn't expected. Still, Penny wouldn't have it any other way.

As the party began to wind down, Penny moved through the room, thanking each guest as they left. The decorations still hung from the ceiling, casting soft shadows in the dim light, and Penny couldn't help but pause in the living room, taking in the scene around her. These people—her parents, her friends—they had been her lifeline through some of the hardest moments in her life. She loved them all fiercely, grateful for the way they had shaped her into the person she was today.

Once the house was settled and the kids were asleep, Penny made her way back to Nathan, who was already waiting for her in the living room. She slipped her arms around him from behind, resting her head against his back. He turned in her arms, pulling her close and pressing a kiss to the top of her head.

"When you came back from Seattle that day," Penny began softly, her voice barely above a whisper, "did you ever imagine any of this?"

Nathan pulled back slightly, his eyes searching hers. "Honestly? I don't think I could have imagined anything this amazing," he said, his voice warm with sincerity. "I know it sounds cheesy, but after everything we went through, I feel like we've come out stronger. I mean, look at us—we've got two incredible kids, a life we built together, and we're still laughing through it all."

Penny smiled, her eyes shimmering. "We really are lucky, aren't we?" she whispered, taking his hand in hers and lacing their fingers together.

Nathan's gaze softened as he looked at her, his thumb gently brushing over her knuckles. "More than lucky," he murmured. "I'm grateful every single day that we found each other in that bar."

Penny laughed softly, the memory of their first meeting replaying in her mind. It seemed so long ago, and yet, here they were—stronger, happier, and filled with love. And she owed it all to that one crazy night of karaoke—when fate had nudged her in the right direction, guiding her toward the life she never knew she needed but now couldn't imagine living without.

She tugged gently on his hand, leading him toward their bedroom. "We've come a long way, haven't we?"

Nathan nodded, following her lead, his heart full. "Yeah," he whispered, pulling her close as they climbed into bed. "And the best part is, we're just getting started."

Dear Reader

Your trust in me and your decision to spend your precious time reading this book hold a special place in my heart. Writing is more than a passion for me, it's a deep-seated love that drives me to create captivating stories of hope and rediscovering through later-in-life and second chance romances. But what truly ignites my soul is the connection I share with readers like you and the invaluable feedback you provide.

If you found the story enjoyable, I would be incredibly grateful if you could spare just a minute to leave a review on Amazon. Your support would mean the world to me, and I genuinely look forward to hearing your thoughts. Your words have the power to uplift and inspire me, and I'm excitedly waiting to learn from your feedback.

Sending you sandy hugs and sunny smiles!

XOXO

Kel Summers

Click here to leave a review on Amazon
Click here to leave a review on BookBub
Click here to leave a review on GoodReads

About Kel Summers

Kel Summers writes clean women's fiction romance books with a focus on later-in-life and second-chance love. Her writing captures the essence of hope, self-discovery, and growth, resonating deeply with readers who appreciate stories of love and new beginnings.

Her personal journey, fueled by her own struggles and heart-breaking loss, led her to leave behind her life in Georgia and venture to the peaceful shores of the Florida Keys. It was there that she found solace, inspiration, and the courage to pursue her lifelong dream of becoming an author.

With her toes in the sand, a pen in her hand, and her faithful and furry canine companion Ivy by her side, she creates tales of love, resilience, and the power of second chances. Through her books, Kel offers readers a chance to escape into beautiful and peaceful coastal settings, where her characters experience personal growth, rekindle lost passions, and find love when they least expect it.

Kel Summers' books resonate with readers seeking heartwarming stories that transport them to the beach, where love and new beginnings flourish. Her clean and uplifting romances capture the beauty of later-in-life love and the profound impact it can have on one's life. With each new release, Kel continues to captivate readers and remind them that, no matter the challenges faced, there is always an opportunity for healing and a second chance at finding true happiness.

Discover the healing power of second chances and the magic of love in Kel Summers' later-in-life, women's fiction, clean beach romances.

Follow me on Amazon at https://www.amazon.com/stores/Kel-Summers/author/B0C74QG5L7

***

Follow me on Facebook at https://www.facebook.com/KelSummersRomanceAuthor

Books by Kel Summers

https://linktr.ee/kelsummers

Click on the links below to learn more about each title.

Shores of Sunset Cove

Silent Sunsets
Exclusive Freebie

Waves of Change
Shores of Sunset Cove Book 1

Tides of Change
Shores of Sunset Cove Book 2

Eve of Change
Shores of Sunset Cove Book 3

Shores of Change
Shores of Sunset Cove Book 4

Summer of Change
Shores of Sunset Cove Book 5

§

Seaside Dreams & Wishing Wells

Summer in Carmel
Exclusive Freebie

Return to Carmel
Seaside Dreams & Wishing Wells Book 1

Conflict in Carmel

Seaside Dreams & Wishing Wells Book 2

Secrets in Carmel
Seaside Dreams & Wishing Wells Book 3

Wedding in Carmel
Seaside Dreams & Wishing Wells Book 4

Second Chances in Carmel
Seaside Dreams & Wishing Wells Book 5

Forever in Carmel
Seaside Dreams & Wishing Wells Book 6

§

The Lighthouse Cove Series

Lighthouse Promises
The Lighthouse Cove Series Book 1

Shadows of the Past
The Lighthouse Cove Series Book 2

The Future of Forever
The Lighthouse Cove Series Book 3

Heartache & Happiness
The Lighthouse Cove Series Book 4

Windswept Promises
The Lighthouse Cove Series Book 5

§

On Air Series

Change for a Penny
On Air Book 1

A Penny for Your Thoughts
On Air Book 2

Picking up the Pennies
On Air Book 3

Pennies and Possibilities
On Air Book 4

Made in United States
North Haven, CT
15 July 2025

70716061R00085